ITALIAN
MADE EASY
LEVEL 2

*An Intermediate Italian Workbook
To Build Essential Vocabulary And Grammar With Ease
(Italian Audio Lessons Included)*

LingoMastery

ISBN: 978-1-951949-86-0

Copyright © 2025 by Lingo Mastery

ALL RIGHTS RESERVED

No part of this book may be reproduced, stored in a retrieval system, or transmitted in any form or by any means, electronic, mechanical, photocopying, recording, scanning, or otherwise, without prior written permission from the publisher.

The illustrations in this book were designed using images from Freepik.com.

CONTENTS

Preface / About the Language 1

Structure 3

Introduction 4

HOW TO GET THE AUDIO FILES 5

UNIT 1 - READY, SET, GO! 6

   Chapter 1 – The Present Progressive Tense 7

      Exercises I 11

   Chapter 2 – The House, Pt. 1 13

      Exercises II 15

   Chapter 3 – The Imperfect Tense 17

      Exercises III 20

   Chapter 4 – School 22

      Exercises IV 25

   Extra – Italian songs 26

UNIT 2 – DIVING INTO THE LANGUAGE 30

   Chapter 1 – Talking About the Future 31

      Exercises I 38

   Chapter 2 – The House, Pt. 2 40

      Exercises II 43

   Chapter 3 – Personality 44

      Exercises III 47

   Chapter 4 – Future Perfect 48

      Exercises IV 51

Chapter 5 – The Human Body, Pt. 1 52
Exercises V 55
Extra – Italian songs 56

UNIT 3 – RUNNING TOWARD FLUENCY 62
Chapter 1 – Demonstrative Adjectives 63
Exercises I 66
Chapter 2 – The House, Pt. 3 67
Exercises II 69
Chapter 3 – The Imperative Mood 70
Exercises III 74
Chapter 4 – Computing and IT 75
Exercises IV 79
Extra – Italian songs 81

UNIT 4 – EXPERIENCING EVERYDAY LIFE 86
Chapter 1 – The Past Perfect Tense 87
Exercises I 91
Chapter 2 – The House, Pt. 4 92
Exercises II 94
Chapter 3 – Active and Passive Voice 95
Exercises III 101
Chapter 4 – Work and Festivities 103
Exercises IV 108
Extra – Italian songs 110

UNIT 5 – TALKING LIKE A LOCAL 116

Chapter 1 – Demonstrative Pronouns 117
Exercises I 120

Chapter 2 – The Human Body, Pt. 2 121
Exercises II 123

Chapter 3 – Ordinal Numbers 124
Exercises III 127

Chapter 4 – The House, Pt. 5 128
Exercises IV 130

Chapter 5 – The Lingo 131

Extra – Italian songs 136

Conclusion 141
Illustrated Guide to Italian Gestures 143
Irregular Past Participles 144
False Friends 145
Answer Key 147

PREFACE
ABOUT THE LANGUAGE

As you may already know, the Italian language comes from ancient Latin, but not the classical form. When we talk about "classical" Latin, we refer to the language spoken by Cicero, Julius Caesar, Augustus, and all the most famous writers, philosophers, and emperors during the time of the Roman Empire.

In fact, the development of the Italian language started after the fall of the Roman Empire, in the 5th century AD, with the beginning of a new era: *the Middle Ages* – or **il Medioevo**, in Italian.

From that century, the so-called *vulgar* language – coming from the Latin **volgo**, *the people,* hence the language spoken by the people – started to spread across modern Europe. This is why such European languages as Spanish, French, Portuguese, and Romanian share so many similarities. They all have the same roots, represented by vulgar Latin.

However, we will have to wait until the 13th century to see more written documents in Italian. Think of Dante, who started writing his **Divina Commedia** at the beginning of the 14th century.

Coming back to the present, over 60 million people in the world people speak Italian. Furthermore, over 3 million speak Italian as their second language. As expected, most of these Italian speakers live in Italy, but there are huge communities of Italians in South America, especially in Argentina, Venezuela, Brazil, and in North America – because of the migrations in the last century – and also in Croatia, Slovenia, and Albania.

Each one of Italy's twenty regions has its own dialect, which was created by the influence of the several waves of invasions that prevailed in the different areas. However, since you are learning the "standard" Italian, you do *not* have to worry. Everyone in Italy will understand you, no matter where you are.

And even if you feel like your Italian is not good enough – yet – it is important to review and/or study at least a few words and expressions before traveling to Italy. If you are going to the biggest cities, it is likely that you will come across Italians who speak English – especially the younger generations – but a bit of Italian always comes in handy and is definitely necessary if you are planning on staying in smaller cities or in less touristic ones.

What happens if you want to speak in Italian, but you forgot the translation of certain words? Hand gestures are the key! Those are part of the language itself, and you will discover that they can also be very helpful to express yourself when words fail. *And yeeees!* As we want you to be as fluent and confident as possible, we added a very self-explanatory guide to Italian gestures at the end of the workbook.

With this workbook, we aim to help you deepen your knowledge of this fascinating language, and make you feel more confident with your own skills.

STRUCTURE

Learning a language is always challenging, but it should also be a fun and rewarding experience. The aim of this book is to offer you a self-taught course of study that will allow you to understand this language better, as well as the culture to which it belongs.

This book will provide you with the linguistic, cultural, and strategic tools to communicate in Italian. The learning path has been carefully planned so that the student can develop a more personal experience while practicing the language.

Each chapter is dedicated to a specific topic required to be fluent in Italian. Some of them are more focused on grammar, while others are centered on useful vocabulary and how-to situations, so that you have all the tools you need to start navigating this fascinating language.

The exercises following each section are designed to reinforce what has been learned, while allowing you to expand the vocabulary.

 This headphone symbol next to a paragraph or dialogue indicates that audio content is available for the corresponding section.

 This headphone with a pencil next to an exercise means that you will need to refer to the corresponding audio content to complete the exercise.

Ready to continue learning Italian in an easy, fun way?

Iniziamo! *Let's start!*

INTRODUCTION

Far from being a comprehensive book covering everything about the Italian language, with this book we want to give you the tools you need to start speaking and understanding the Italian language right away. We will review and further study what we taught you with the first book of this series.

Of course, the first rule is: **take your time** while exploring the different sections of the workbook – do not rush through them, but rather enjoy this journey into the Italian language.

This book is aimed at people of all ages who want to start learning Italian, or people who have already been studying the language and want to refresh their skills. It will cover the basics of the level A2-B1 in the Common European Framework of Reference for Languages (CEFR).

We want to give you the tools you need to expand your knowledge and improve your skills.

Try completing all the exercises, as they are structured not only to make you practice what you are learning in that given section, but also to consolidate words and rules throughout the whole book.

In order to keep you motivated, we included extra sections at the end of each unit with the lyrics of some Italian songs that we will analyze together. You may know some of them already, and you may have never heard of others. These songs will not only enrich your vocabulary, but they will also provide you with an insight into the Italian culture – and maybe you will also discover a few new songs that you like!

If there is anything we have learned from the Italians, **it is to go with the flow**, enjoy simple things, and take a break whenever you feel you need one!

Andrai alla grande!
You will do a great job!

HOW TO GET THE AUDIO FILES

Some of the exercises throughout this book come with accompanying audio files. You can download these audio files if you head over to:

www.lingomastery.com/italian-me2-audio

If you're having trouble downloading the audio, contact us at

www.lingomastery.com/contact

UNIT 1
READY, SET, GO!

CHAPTER 1
THE PRESENT PROGRESSIVE TENSE

You have just opened this new book, you are fresh, you are motivated... so why not start with some grammar? Do not worry, though, we do not mean to scare you... *hopefully*.

In this chapter, we are going to focus on the present progressive tense. Maybe this definition does not mean much to you, but we are *very* sure that you know what we are talking about. In English, the present progressive tense has the following structure:

subject pronoun + to be + main verb with -ing ending

It is a tense that we commonly use to describe a situation in progress, a situation that is happening *right now*. For example: *I am writing a workbook on the Italian language*.

Please note that, in English, the same structure is used for the future progressive tense, meaning that it is used to refer to a **future** action or event that has been previously planned. For example, *I am going to the hairdresser's tomorrow at 4 p.m.* In Italian, the future tense has a completely different structure. In this chapter, then, we will explain how to form this tense to talk about something that is happening right now.

First, let's talk about the differences with the corresponding English tense. If you remember, in Italian, subject pronouns are rarely used because the conjugated verb indicates who the subject is. In short, the sentence *I am writing a book* would simply become *am writing a book* in Italian.

As there is not a subject pronoun, the Italian present progressive – **il presente progressivo** – is made of two elements. However, they are not the same ones as in English.

The conjugated auxiliary *to be* is replaced by the Italian auxiliary verb **stare,** which is going to be conjugated in the present tense. Funnily enough, when it is used as a "normal" verb, the verb **stare** means *to stay*.

Stare is a regular verb belonging to the **-are** group of verbs. We remind you that, in Italian, there are three verb groups: **-are, -ere, -ire**, whose conjugations are slightly different.

Because **fa sempre bene ripassare** – *it is always good to review things* – let's take a look at the conjugation of this auxiliary verb in the present tense.

io	sto
tu	stai
lui/lei/Lei	sta
noi	stiamo
voi	state
loro	stanno

As you can see, the verb is almost regular, as we have the verb root – **st-** – followed by the corresponding endings of the present tense. The only tiny exceptions are for the subject pronouns **tu** and **loro**, where we have to add an extra *a* and an additional *n* to the verb endings, respectively.

The *-ing* form of the main verb is replaced by the so-called **gerundio** form. It is as simple as in English, though. The gerundio form is an invariable one, meaning that you will not have to conjugate it, and you do not have to adapt it according to gender and number of the subject to which it refers. Good news, right?

So, how do we form this tense?

This is how you do it for each verb group:

- **-are** group: We take the verb root – i.e., the part of the infinitive form without the -are ending – and we add the suffix **-ando**.
  Examples: mangiare-mangiando, cantare-cantando, lavare-lavando, etc.

- **-ere** group: We add the suffix **-endo** to the verb root.
  Examples: vedere-vedendo, prendere-prendendo, togliere-togliendo, etc.

- **-ire** group: We add the suffix **-endo** to the verb root, as we do for the -ere group.
  Examples: capire-capendo, venire-venendo, salire-salendo, etc.

Well, as you may expect, there are a few irregular verbs... but not many! The most important verbs with an irregular **gerundio** form are **dire-dicendo, fare-facendo** and **bere-bevendo**, the verbs *to say, to do/make,* and *to drink,* respectively.

This is literally all we have to say about the **gerundio** form!

Now, let's put together everything we have said so far. The most common question one may ask using the present progressive tense is probably: "*What are you doing?*"

When translating this question into Italian, you just have to remember not to use the subject pronoun, to replace the auxiliary *to be* with **stare** conjugated in the present tense, and to make the **gerundio** form of the verb *to do*, which – we remind you – is one of three irregular verbs indicated just above.

The result is the question **che cosa stai facendo?**

Of course, in this instance, the subject pronoun would not be needed in any case because I am addressing just one person, *you*, specifically. The subject is often made explicit when it is a personal name, for example, **Giulia sta andando a scuola** – *Giulia is going to school*.

What happens when we want to use a reflexive or a reciprocal verb, though?

As a reminder, reflexive verbs are those verbs whose subject and object are the same. For example, *he washes himself*. In English, they can also be expressed with the verb *get*, as in, for example, *they get angry*. Reciprocal verbs, on the other hand, express an action involving two people. For example, *they hug each other*.

If you remember, the main thing you must not forget, when using these verbs in Italian, is to add the reflexive pronoun. So if there is no reflexive pronoun, then it is not a reflexive verb. Before moving forward, let's quickly review the reflexive pronouns:

myself	mi
yourself	ti
himself/herself/itself	si
ourselves	ci
yourselves	vi
themselves	si

The same rule applies when you are planning on conjugating reflexive or reciprocal verbs in the present progressive tense. You MUST use the reflexive pronoun with this tense as well, and it will go right before the conjugated form of **stare**. For example, **ci stiamo preparando** – *we are getting ready*.

To finish this chapter, we will show you a few examples of common sentences and situations requiring the present progressive tense:

Examples:

- **Dov'è Patrizia?**
  Sta uscendo proprio adesso.
  Where is Patrizia?
  She is going out just now.

- **Sto passando l'aspirapolvere, altrimenti mia moglie si arrabbia.**
  I am vacuuming, otherwise, my wife will get angry.
  (A great example, and also a big truth!)

- **A cosa stai pensando?**
  What are you thinking about?

With this last example, you can see a difference in terms of prepositions. When it comes to phrasal verbs – verbs followed by a specific preposition, like *to think <u>about</u>* – in questions, the Italian preposition goes at the beginning of the question itself, and not at the end of it as in English.

- **Stiamo preparando il dolce per il compleanno di Francesca.**
  We are making the cake for Francesca's birthday.

We would like to remind you that, in Italian, the English possessive does not exist. A construction like *Francesca's birthday* always needs to be expressed as *the birthday <u>of</u> Francesca*, thus requiring the Italian preposition **di**.

- **Ti stai annoiando?**
  Are you getting bored?

(Note: As you are reading/studying this workbook, the answer to this question should always be "no.")

 EXERCISES I

1) Scrivi i seguenti verbi al gerundio. *Change the following verbs to the gerundio form.*

a) asciugare _____

b) chiamare _____

c) bere _____

d) guardare _____

e) finire _____

f) avere _____

g) fare _____

h) scrivere _____

i) sentire _____

2) Visto che ci siamo... *While we are at it... Write the English translation of the verbs from the exercise above.*

a) asciugare _____

b) chiamare _____

c) bere _____

d) guardare _____

e) finire _____

f) avere _____

g) fare _____

h) scrivere _____

i) sentire _____

3) Che cosa stai facendo? *What are you doing? Answer the question and use as much vocabulary as possible.*

CHAPTER 2
THE HOUSE, PT. 1

This chapter will focus on daily vocabulary... the vocabulary related to the house!

Please note that this is just the first part of our *house series*. In this first chapter, we want to discuss all the vocabulary/topics related to the house in general, whereas we will focus on the details of each room in the next sections.

First, in Italian, there is just one word to describe the place in which you live – **casa** – so you do not have two options like in English (*house/home*). On the other hand, the word **casa** is rather generic, and there are different kinds of houses / buildings. Look at the list below:

appartamento	*apartment*
monolocale	*studio apartment*
bilocale	*two-room apartment*
trilocale	*three-room apartment*
villetta	*small villa*
villa	*villa*
palazzo	*building*
grattacielo	*skyscraper*
attico	*penthouse*

Now you know how to describe the place in which you live. What about adding more information?

As you may already know, in Italy people use *square meters* – **metri quadrati** – as a unit of measure to express the surface of a property.

In a building, there are several *floors*, or **piani,** the plural form of **piano** (yes, it is the same word as the musical instrument). As in English, when mentioning an apartment floor, for example, you will have to use ordinal numbers, and not cardinal ones – i.e., **primo piano, secondo piano, terzo piano,** etc. We discussed ordinal numbers in the first book, so do not hesitate to go back and have a look if you feel like you need to revisit this topic.

Moving forward, it is also important to know how to say that you are a tenant. In this instance, the sentence you would use is **sono in affitto**. Otherwise, if you are a house/apartment owner, you will say **sono proprietario/a** – masculine/feminine, respectively.

Inside the house, there can be one or more **stanze** – *rooms*. Let's look at the Italian names of the rooms and spaces within a house.

ingresso	*entrance*	**camera da letto**	*bedroom*
corridoio	*corridor*	**studio**	*study/office*
scale	*staircase*	**bagno**	*bathroom*
balcone	*balcony*	**ripostiglio**	*storage/utility room*
terrazza	*terrace*	**lavanderia**	*laundry room*
cucina	*kitchen*	**soffitta**	*attic*
salotto	*living room*	**cantina**	*cellar*
sala da pranzo	*dining room*	**garage**	*garage*

Outside the house/apartment, there may be a *garden* – **un giardino** – or a *courtyard*, too – **un cortile**.

Now let's look at some essential elements inside a property:

muri/pareti	*walls*
tetto	*roof*
soffitto	*ceiling*
pavimento	*floor*
finestra	*window*
porta	*door*

Well, now you know all the vocabulary that is needed to talk about properties.

Ready to put all of this into practice?

📝 EXERCISES II

1) **Scrivi i nomi delle stanze in italiano.** *Write the Italian names of the rooms.*

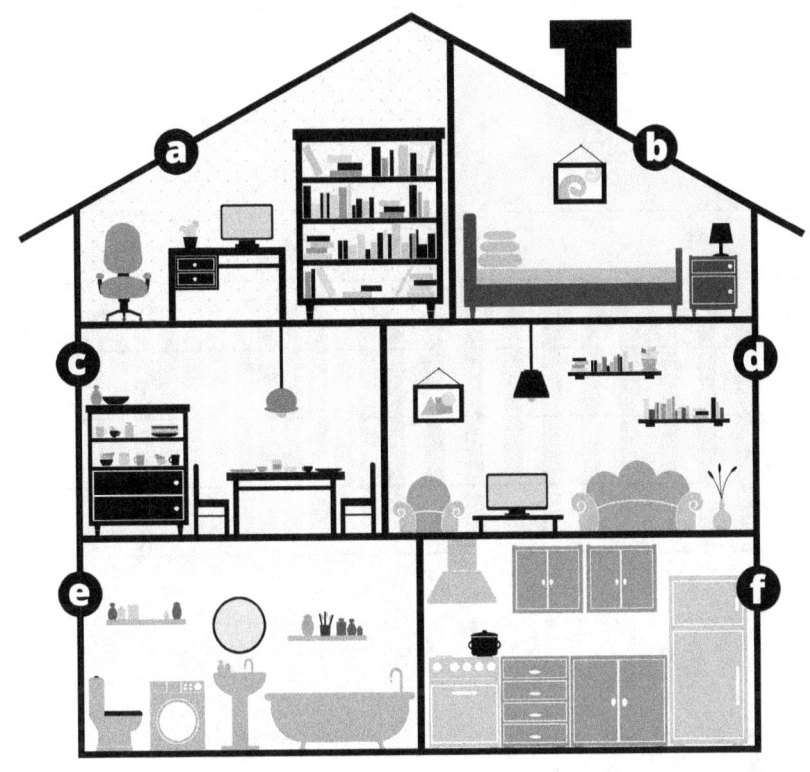

a) _____   d) _____

b) _____   e) _____

c) _____   f) _____

2) **Ascolta l'audio.** *Listen to the audio file and add the missing words in the text. There may be more than just one word for each blank space.* (Find audio on page 5.)

Finalmente _____ casa! Eravamo _____ da ormai cinque anni.

Avevamo un _____ molto carino in centro, non lontano dalla stazione. Anche se

non era _____ , ci siamo sempre sentiti a casa. Ora che la mia ragazza è

incinta, ci serviva un'altra _____ . Il mio sogno è sempre stato quello di avere

un _____ , e sono davvero contento che la nostra nuova casa lo abbia!

_____ di trasferirci.

3) Com'è la tua casa dei sogni? Descrivila. *What does your dream house look like? Describe it using all the vocabulary you have just learned.*

_____
_____
_____
_____
_____
_____
_____
_____
_____
_____

CHAPTER 3
THE IMPERFECT TENSE

In the previous book, we talked about the Italian past tense. We introduced and explained the so-called **passato prossimo**, which corresponds to the *simple past*, even though its structure looks like the English present perfect.

If you remember, the passato prossimo is made of the following elements:

(subject) + auxiliary verb (**avere** or **essere**) + past participle of the main verb

Just like in English, there are regular and irregular past participles. You will find a list of the most common ones at the end of the workbook.

A few examples of sentences with the passato prossimo requiring *to be* or *to have* as the auxiliary verb:

Examples:

- **Ieri ho mangiato al ristorante.** *Yesterday, I ate at the restaurant.*
- **Siamo andati in ufficio alle 9.** *We went to the office at 9.*
- **Hai visto l'ultimo episodio?** *Did you watch the last episode?*

Well, the trick is that... the passato prossimo is not the only simple past in Italian. Actually, there are two main past tenses: the passato prossimo and the so-called **imperfetto**. What is the difference between these two, then?

Even if in English the *imperfect tense* does not exist, the difference from the simple past is not very difficult to understand. In fact, the imperfect tense should be used when we are talking about a regular / ongoing action in the past – for example a habit –, as opposed to a single event / situation, which started and finished in the past.

For example, when you are talking about your experiences at school, it is likely that you will have to use the imperfect tense, as you're describing situations / events that used to happen on a regular basis, and not just once. On the other hand, if you want to talk about something you did last weekend, you will probably use the simple past, as you are describing something that happened only once, at a precise moment in time.

To help you better understand this, you need to use the imperfect with:

- Continuous actions in the past. For example, if you want to say *I used to play the piano three times a week*.

- Feelings and emotions, for example, when translating a sentence like *I was feeling well / badly / anxious / happy*, etc.

- Habits, repeated, regular events, as in *I always woke up at 8:30*.

- After **mentre** – *while*. For example, if you want to say *My friend arrived while I was getting ready*, the first sentence – *my friend arrived* – will have the passato prossimo, and the second one – *while I was getting ready* – with the verb *to be* conjugated in the imperfect tense.

We know that it may seem like a lot to process, and maybe you are already thinking: *Should I really analyze a situation that much, before choosing the right tense?*

Well, the answer is yes, at least at the beginning. Just give yourself time to become familiar with this tense, and you will see that, with time, you will be able to use passato prossimo and imperfetto in the right way without even thinking about it.

Looking forward to some good news?

The imperfect tense is probably the most regular tense *ever*. All students love it. And now you will understand why.

First, we need to explain how to form this tense. You will have to take the verb root – the part of the verb without the ending related to its infinitive – then attach the endings corresponding to this tense.

E sai cosa? *And you know what?*

The endings are almost the same for the three groups!

As you will see in a minute, the "signature" consonant of this tense is letter **V**, which is going to be repeated throughout the verb conjugation. In the table below, you will find the endings of the imperfect tense with the conjugation of three verbs – one for each group.

We have broken down the first conjugated verb in order to show you the two building blocks we have just mentioned:

soggetto	pagare *to pay*	tenere *to keep*	dormire *to sleep*
io	pag-avo	ten-evo	dorm-ivo
tu	pagavi	tenevi	dormivi
lui/lei/Lei	pagava	teneva	dormiva
noi	pagavamo	tenevamo	dormivamo
voi	pagavate	tenevate	dormivate
loro	pagavano	tenevano	dormivano

On the other hand, there are also a few irregular verbs. But there are just a few of them. You will find the most used ones in the table below.

soggetto	essere *to be*	fare *to do*	bere *to drink*	dire *to say*
io	ero	facevo	bevevo	dicevo
tu	eri	facevi	bevevi	dicevi
lui/lei/Lei	era	faceva	beveva	diceva
noi	eravamo	facevamo	bevevamo	dicevamo
voi	eravate	facevate	bevevate	dicevate
loro	erano	facevano	bevevano	dicevano

Of course, we can conjugate reflexive and reciprocal verbs in the imperfect tense. The only thing you will have to do – besides conjugating the verb itself – is add the reflexive pronoun in front of it.

Before starting to practice with some exercises, let's look at a few examples of sentences with the imperfect tense alone, or along with the simple past.

Examples:

- **Cantavo sempre sotto la doccia.** — *I always used to sing in the shower.*
- **Anche se era stanca, è venuta.** — *She came even though she was tired.*
- **Ballavano a ogni festa.** — *They danced at every party.*

Please note that we could reverse the order of the two clauses of the second example – **è venuta anche se era stanca** – and the meaning would remain the same.

EXERCISES III

1) Imperfetto o passato prossimo? *Write whether you have to use the imperfect tense (I) or the simple past (SP) when translating the following sentences in Italian. Please note that there may be two verbs.*

   a) We used to go on holiday to Italy.   _____

   b) Yesterday he bought a car.   _____

   c) She came, even though if she was very busy.   _____   _____

   d) You watched an action movie.   _____

   e) You woke up at 6 every day.   _____

   f) Last year, I graduated.   _____

   g) Did she see her boss today?   _____

2) Coniuga i verbi all'imperfetto. *Conjugate the following verbs in the imperfect tense. Beware! There may be irregular and reflexive verbs.*

soggetto	sedersi to sit	vendere to sell	essere to be	fermare to stop
io				
tu				
lui/lei/Lei				
noi				
voi				
loro				

3) Ascolta l'audio. *Listen to the audio file and add the missing verbs.* (Find audio on page 5.)

Quando _____ un adolescente, _____ imparare l'inglese a ogni costo. _____ che mi sarebbe stato utile, e in più _____ viaggiare. _____ di riuscire a farmi capire ovunque andassi. _____ sodo ogni giorno, e devo ammettere che non _____ facile. _____ la mattina e _____ la sera, esausto. _____ dire di essere molto fiero di me perchè adesso _____ benissimo l'inglese.

Translation

When I was a teenager, I wanted to learn English at all costs. I knew that it would be useful, and I loved traveling as well. I hoped to be able to make myself understood wherever I went. I studied hard every day, and I have to admit that it has not been easy. I started in the morning and ended in the evening, exhausted. I can say that I am very proud of myself because now I speak English very well.

CHAPTER 4
SCHOOL

Well, well, well.

It is now time to talk about something that could be one of your fondest memories or a nightmare... *school* – **la scuola**.

In this chapter, we want to introduce a lot of new words that will be helpful even if you are no longer in school. In fact, we use many of the following words in our everyday life as well.

In the first book, we discussed how the school system works in Italy, so we do not want to repeat ourselves and be boring. However, if you have not read the first book – *really????* – let's just summarize how the Italian school system is organized:

5 years of *primary school* - **scuola elementare** – followed by 3 years of *middle school* – **scuola media** – followed by 5 years of *high school* – **scuola superiore.**

In Italy, *grades* – **i voti** – go from 1 to 10, meaning that you will have to get at least a 6 to pass the test.

Compared to other school systems, it can be surprising to find out that Italian students never change their *classroom* – **la classe**. Students use the same classroom every day and they stay there until the day is over. In short, the *teachers* – **gli insegnanti** – are those who go from one classroom to the other.

Let's learn the Italian names of school subjects:

matematica	*math*
fisica	*physics*
storia	*history*
geografia	*geography*
scienze	*science*
letteratura	*literature*
educazione fisica	*P.E.*

tecnologia	*technology*
arte	*art*
educazione civica	*civic education*
musica	*music*

Not all these subjects are taught in the same school cycle. For example, civic education is taught in primary school. On the other hand, most Italian students have their music lessons in middle school only. Unless they are in a school specializing in music, they can generally choose between a few instruments: *keyboards, guitar, flute* – **tastiera, chitarra, flauto,** respectively. It is also up to the parents to buy the musical instruments for those lessons.

Now, let's get *inside* a classroom. Here's a list of the most common elements:

banco	*school desk*
cattedra	*teacher's desk*
lavagna	*blackboard*
zaino	*backpack*
astuccio	*pencil case*
matita	*pencil*
gomma	*rubber*
matita colorata	*colored pencil*
penna	*pen*
forbici	*scissors*
colla	*glue*
scotch	*tape*
quaderno	*notebook*
appunti	*notes*

As you can see, we do not use the words above only when we talk about school, and this is why we decided that it was time to introduce them.

Oh, right. Another thing that you may not know if you have not studied our first workbook: in Italian schools there are no *lockers* – **armadietti**. Students need to carry all the material they need every single day. This means a student might have to carry a backpack full of books and notebooks, their musical instrument, the bag with all the things needed for P.E., and sometimes even an additional folder for art lessons!

As per *school hours* – **gli orari scolastici** – we could say that Italian schools generally start at 8:30 and finish between 1:30-2:30. Of course, there are also some schools with lessons in the afternoon, and, in that instance, school ends around 4:30 p.m.

It may seem that Italian students have a lot of free time, but **non è tutto oro quel che luccica** – *all that glitters is not gold*. Italian students have a lot of *homework* – **compiti** – to do every day, and they do not have many breaks during the school year. Besides public holidays, they have time off only for Christmas – a couple of weeks – and Easter – a week.

Generally speaking, the school year ends in the second week of June, as afterward it usually gets too warm and 90% of Italian schools are not equipped with air conditioning!

Well, after focusing on vocabulary, we are now going to challenge you a little with our exercise section. Remember: Challenges are what makes life interesting as they force you to put into practice everything you have learned so far.

Ready to practice your writing skills?

📝 EXERCISES IV

1) Come funziona la scuola nel tuo paese? *How does the school system work in your country? Try to describe it by using all the vocabulary learned so far. Please mention your personal experience, too. For example, what was your favorite subject? Which subject did you not like at all? Why?*

_____
_____
_____
_____
_____
_____
_____
_____

2) Descrivi l'aula. *Describe the classroom you see in the image below.*

_____
_____
_____
_____

EXTRA
ITALIAN SONGS

Our first song section! We hope that you are eager to learn more about some famous – and less famous – Italian songs.

How is this going to work? Easy. First, we will introduce the song lyrics. You will see the Italian lyrics with corresponding translation in English right below every line. Then, we will highlight a few interesting facts about the lyrics themselves, whether they are about the text itself, grammar, vocabulary, or cultural points.

We could not choose a different song to **aprire le danze** – *to get the ball rolling*.

Which song are we talking about? **Azzurro**, of course!

Do not hesitate to listen to the song in the meantime. Try to follow the lyrics first, and then look at their translation.

 Azzurro (Adriano Celentano)   (Find audio on page 5.)

Cerco l'estate tutto l'anno e all'improvviso eccola qua
I'm looking for summer all year round and all of a sudden here it is

Lei è partita per le spiagge e sono solo quassù in città
She left for the beach and I am alone here in town

Sento fischiare sopra i tetti un aeroplano che se ne va
I hear an airplane whistling over the roofs while leaving

Azzurro il pomeriggio è troppo azzurro e lungo per me
Light blue, the afternoon is too light blue and long for me

Mi accorgo di non avere più risorse senza di te
I realize I do not have any more resources without you

E allora io quasi quasi prendo il treno e vengo, vengo da te
And then I could take the train and come, come to you

Ma il treno dei desideri nei miei pensieri all'incontrario va
But the desire train in my thoughts goes the other way

Sembra quand'ero all'oratorio con tanto sole, tanti anni fa
It seems when I was at the oratory with so much sun, so many years ago

Quelle domeniche da solo in un cortile, a passeggiar
Those Sundays alone in a courtyard, walking

Ora mi annoio più di allora neanche un prete per chiacchierar
Now I get bored more than then, there is not even a priest to talk to

Azzurro il pomeriggio è troppo azzurro e lungo per me
Light blue, the afternoon is too light blue and long for me

Mi accorgo di non avere più risorse senza di te
I realize I do not have any more resources without you

E allora io quasi quasi prendo il treno e vengo, vengo da te
And then I could take the train and come, come to you

Ma il treno dei desideri nei miei pensieri all'incontrario va
But the desire train in my thoughts goes the other way

Cerco un po' d'Africa in giardino, tra l'oleandro e il baobab
I'm looking for a bit of Africa in the garden, between the oleander and the baobab

Come facevo da bambino, ma qui c'è gente, non si può più
Like I used to do as a child, but there are people here, you cannot do it anymore

Stanno innaffiando le tue rose, non c'è il leone, chissà dov'è
They are watering your roses, there is no lion, who knows where it is

Azzurro il pomeriggio è troppo azzurro e lungo per me
Light blue, the afternoon is too light blue and long for me

Mi accorgo di non avere più risorse senza di te
I realize I do not have any more resources without you

How did it go? Was it easy or difficult to follow the song while reading the lyrics?

In case you asked yourself some questions when you were reading the English translation, well... just remember that it is a song. The lyrics do not always make sense, and this song may be a good example of it.

What is this story about? It is the story of a man in love who remained in the city while his girlfriend left to go to the seaside. You may think that she left him because maybe he had to work and could not join her.

If you remember what he said, though – **Ora mi annoio più di allora neanche un prete per chiacchierar** – this guy is *reeeally* bored and he does not even have a job to help him kill the time. She has just left him. In short, they broke up.

Also, what is wrong with the **treno dei desideri** – *the desire train*? Why is it going the other way? Another sad answer... because this guy cannot have back what he lost.

As per the part about Africa... please do not ask us about it. We have no idea.

It is probably a sadder song than you expected, right? But still, it is one of the most famous Italian songs, and one of those that everyone knows. We promise that next song will be more cheerful.

To finish this extra section, here are some interesting facts about vocabulary:

quasi quasi: quasi quasi is a very common way to say that you are thinking about doing something that is appealing to you. Even though there is not a precise translation, we could translate it in English as *half tempted*.

eccola qua: translated as *here it is*, please note that the **eccola** has been adapted to the feminine version – see the final *a* – because it refers to **l'estate** – *summer* – which is a feminine singular word in Italian. In everyday life, to say *here it is*, it is more common to say just **ecco!**, which is also invariable.

mi accorgo: please note that there are two possible translations of the English verb *to realize* – **realizzare,** which is a "normal" verb, and **accorgersi**, which is a reflexive one, as it has been used here.

un po': translated as *a bit*, why that weird apostrophe at the end? Because **po'** is actually the "trimmed" version of the word **poco**. Italians do not say **un poco** anymore, so you should always say **un po'**. Do not forget that apostrophe! Humorously enough, the word Po, with capital letter and no apostrophe, is the name of the longest river in Italy.

chissà: common translation for *who knows*.

To finish this section, if you feel like you would like to revisit what you have learned so far, we suggest underlining all the verbs that you see in the lyrics. You will soon realize that they are all conjugated in tenses that you have studied.

We hope that you enjoyed this extra section, and we are looking forward to introducing the next one! **Non barare, però** – *However, do not cheat.*

We know that your **treno dei desideri** would bring you directly to the next song, but you should see it as a final reward after having studied our next chapters!

UNIT 2
DIVING INTO THE LANGUAGE

CHAPTER 1
TALKING ABOUT THE FUTURE

We started Unit 1 with a chapter on a verb tense, so why not do the same for this new one?

To recap, now you know how to use conjugated verbs for current situations/events and those in the past– that is already a big accomplishment! What are we missing here, then?

Obviously, the next step is learning how to use the *future tense*. In English, there are four main ways to talk about future events:

- *Simple present*, for scheduled events/actions. For example, *The bus leaves at 4:30*.

- *Present continuous*, for plans and arrangements. For example, *I am going to the bank tomorrow*.

- *To be going to*, for future intentions that are not "scheduled." For example, *This weekend he is going to visit his aunt*.

- *Will*, for predictions, beliefs, intentions, promises and offers. For example, *Lunch will be on us the next time we meet*.

Good news!

In Italian, there is just one way to talk about the future. Well, technically, you can use the simple present, but it is usually better to use the *future tense* – **il futuro semplice**.

However, there are some instances where you'd use the future tense in English, and the simple present in Italian.

Examples:

- **Offro io!**   *I will pay!*
- **Apro io la porta.**   *I will open the door.*

Now, moving on to the verb conjugation. Once again, the first building block is the verb root. Then, you will have to attach the corresponding endings related to the future tense in Italian. Look at the three examples of verbs – one for each group – conjugated in the future tense on the next page.

soggetto	chiamare *to call*	crescere *to grow*	condire *to season*
io	chiam-erò	cresc-erò	cond-irò
tu	chiamerai	crescerai	condirai
lui/lei/Lei	chiamerà	crescerà	condirà
noi	chiameremo	cresceremo	condiremo
voi	chiamerete	crescerete	condirete
loro	chiameranno	cresceranno	condiranno

Have you noticed anything regarding the conjugation of the two **-are** and **-ere** verbs in the future tense?

Yes, the endings are the same! **-erò, -erai, -erà, -eremo, -erete, -eranno**, respectively. Also, the endings of the **-ire** verbs are not that different – it's just the *i* replacing the *e* of the other endings. *Thank you, Italian grammar.*

Let's now look at a few examples of sentences with the future tense.

Examples:

- **Domani comprerò un nuovo divano.** *Tomorrow I will buy a new couch.*
- **L'anno prossimo cambierà casa.** *Next year he/she will move house.*

On the other hand, as you may expect, there are some irregular verbs as well. Let's start with the most irregular one, which is – as usual – the verb *to be*, whose verb root changes completely when we conjugate this verb in the future tense.

soggetto	essere *to be*
io	sarò
tu	sarai
lui/lei/Lei	sarà
noi	saremo
voi	sarete
loro	saranno

To show you the main irregularities of the future tense, let's quickly discuss those verbs losing the vowel that joins the verb root and the ending of the future – for example, the *e* of **cresc-erò**. The verb **andare**, *to go*, is probably the best example to introduce this group of irregular verbs.

soggetto	andare *to go*
io	andrò
tu	andrai
lui/lei/Lei	andrà
noi	andremo
voi	andrete
loro	andranno

In fact, if the verb **andare** were a regular one, the translation of *I will go* would be **anderò** – which is super ugly to hear, trust us! The verb loses the *e* before the *r*, and this is how it becomes **andrò**.

The same applies to the following verbs, as well:

avere	*to have*
cadere	*to fall*
dovere	*must/have to*
potere	*can/to be able to*
sapere	*to know*
vedere	*to see*
vivere	*to live*

You will find a few examples of sentences with some of these irregular verbs in the future tense below.

Examples:

- **Domani dovrò fare i compiti.** *Tomorrow I will have to do my homework.*
- **Non cadranno nella trappola.** *They will not fall into the trap.*
- **Vedremo i fuochi d'artificio?** *Are we going to see the fireworks?*

Let's move to the next group of irregular verbs. In this instance, the verb changes its root when conjugated in the future tense. Please note that the same does not necessarily apply when conjugating the same verb in other tenses. In the table below, you will find some of the most common verbs belonging to this group of irregular fellows.

soggetto	volere *to want*	venire *to come*	tenere *to keep*
io	vorrò	verrò	terrò
tu	vorrai	verrai	terrai
lui/lei/Lei	vorrà	verrà	terrà
noi	vorremo	verremo	terremo
voi	vorrete	verrete	terrete
loro	vorranno	verranno	terranno

However, as you can see, the verbs above share a similar conjugation. The stems of these verbs would be **vol-**, **ven-**, and **ten-**, respectively, and when you conjugate them in the future tense, the verb roots change to **vor-**, **ver-**, and **ter-**. Also, as we have seen for the other group of irregular verbs, these verbs lose the vowel before the *r* as well.

Examples:

- **Verranno alla tua festa.** *They will come to your party.*
- **Vorrò una bella macchina.** *I will want a nice car.*
- **Terrai la mano a tuo fratello?** *Will you hold your brother's hand?*

We are almost done, we promise you!

Before finishing this chapter, there are still a couple of exceptions that we need to mention – the Italian verbs ending in **-ciare** or **-giare**. In fact, when we conjugate them in the future tense, they lose the *i* belonging to the verb root. You will find two examples on the next page.

soggetto	mangiare *to eat*	cominciare *to start/to begin*
io	mangerò	comincerò
tu	mangerai	comincerai
lui/lei/Lei	mangerà	comincerà
noi	mangeremo	cominceremo
voi	mangerete	comincerete
loro	mangeranno	cominceranno

In fact, if the verb **mangiare** were a regular one in the future tense, the translation of *I eat* would be **mangierò**, with the *i* belonging to the verb root – **mangi-**.

Look at other examples of verbs ending in **-ciare / -giare**:

lasciare	*to leave*
rinunciare	*to give up/to renounce*
annunciare	*to announce*
baciare	*to kiss*
danneggiare	*to damage*
parcheggiare	*to park*
noleggiare	*to rent (a car, but not an apartment)*
passeggiare	*to walk*
incoraggiare	*to encourage*

And here are a few examples of sentences featuring this verb group:

Examples:

- **Parcheggerai davanti a casa sua?** — *Will you park in front of his place?*
- **Mia madre mi incoraggerà sempre.** — *My mother will always encourage me.*
- **Lasceranno la mancia sul tavolo.** — *They will leave the tip on the table.*

The last thing we should mention concerns those verbs ending with **-care** and **-gare**. When they are conjugated in the future tense, they require the addition of an extra *h* between the verb root and the regular ending of the future. You will find a couple of examples below.

soggetto	pagare *to pay*	cercare *to search/to look for*
io	pagherò	cercherò
tu	pagherai	cercherai
lui/lei/Lei	pagherà	cercherà
noi	pagheremo	cercheremo
voi	pagherete	cercherete
loro	pagheranno	cercheranno

Why do we need that additional *h*, though? It is a pronunciation matter.

If we take into account the infinitive form of the verb to pay, **pagare**, we will read it this way: *pah-gah-reh*. The letter *g* has a hard sound. If we do not add that *h* when conjugating the verb in the future tense, *I will pay* would become **pagerò**, and the pronunciation would change into *pah-jeh-roh*. The pronunciation of the *g* has changed. To keep the original hard sound of the letter, we need that *h*. The result? **Pagherò**, which is read as *pah-gheh-roh*.

The same applies to the **-care** verbs. We add an extra *h* to preserve the hard sound of the letter *c*.

Here's a short list of the most common verbs with a **-care** and **-gare** infinitive:

negare	*to deny*
navigare	*to browse/to navigate*
vagare	*to wander*
allargare	*to widen*
indagare	*to investigate*
pregare	*to pray*
litigare	*to argue*
legare	*to tie*

sporcare	*to dirty*
dimenticare	*to forget*
giocare	*to play (a game or a sport, not a musical instrument)*
sprecare	*to waste*
attaccare	*to attach*
toccare	*to touch*

Let's now finish this section with a few examples of sentences featuring the last verbs we discussed.

Examples:

- **Sprecheranno soltanto il loro tempo.** *They will only waste their time.*
- **Il detective indagherà sul crimine.** *The detective will investigate the crime.*
- **Lo dimenticherò sicuramente!** *I will forget it for sure!*

The last thing we will do – **l'ultima cosa che faremo** – before finishing the whole chapter is add a short list of useful words regarding the future:

domani	*tomorrow*
dopodomani	*the day after tomorrow*
tra due giorni	*in two days*
tra tre anni	*in three years*
l'anno prossimo	*next year*
la settimana prossima	*next week*

The word **prossimo** follows the word it refers to, and it needs to match the gender and the number of the noun to which it refers. For example, we say **l'anno prossimo** as **anno** is a masculine singular word. On the other hand, if we refer to the week – **la settimana** – we must say **prossima,** as it is a feminine singular word.

As promised, this chapter is now over! Take your time to review all the information provided and to practice with our usual exercises.

📝 EXERCISES I

1) Coniuga i seguenti verbi al futuro semplice. *Conjugate the following verbs in the future tense. Beware! There may be some irregular ones.*

soggetto	cucinare	lanciare	credere	essere
io				
tu				
lui/lei/Lei				
noi				
voi				
loro				

2) Traduci i seguenti verbi al futuro semplice. *Translate the following verbs in the future tense.*

a) I will start _____ (cominciare)

b) We will run _____ (correre)

c) You will kiss _____ (baciare, tu)

d) You will come _____ (venire, voi)

e) I will write _____ (scrivere)

f) She will have _____ (avere)

g) He will pray _____ (pregare)

3) Che cosa farai domani? E questo fine settimana? *What will you do tomorrow? And this weekend? Answer the questions using the future tense in Italian. Provide as many details as possible. Remember: practice makes perfect!*

CHAPTER 2
THE HOUSE, PT. 2

In Unit 1 we talked about the house in general terms, and now it is time to explore the different rooms, one at a time. And, of course, since we are learning Italian, the best room to start from has to be the *kitchen*, **la cucina!**

In this chapter, we will focus on the elements that we could find in a kitchen, but not only that. We have a surprise for you at the end of the chapter that we think will be much appreciated.

Without further ado, let's start with the names of the most common household appliances / kitchen tools!

frigorifero	*fridge*	**pentola**	*cooking pot*
congelatore	*freezer*	**coperchio**	*lid*
forno	*oven*	**mestolo**	*ladle*
fornelli	*stove*	**piatto**	*plate*
bollitore	*kettle*	**posate**	*cutlery*
tostapane	*toaster*	**forchetta**	*fork*
microonde	*microwave*	**cucchiaio**	*spoon*
lavastoviglie	*dishwasher*	**coltello**	*knife*
frullatore	*mixer*	**bicchiere**	*glass*
caffettiera/moka	*coffee maker*	**tazza**	*cup*
apriscatole	*can opener*	**tovaglia**	*tablecloth*
cavatappi	*corkscrew*	**tovaglietta**	*placemat*
padella	*pan*	**tovagliolo**	*napkin*

Of course, this is far from being an exhaustive list, but it covers the most important vocabulary you should know when it comes to the kitchen.

Now, as this chapter is essentially focused on vocabulary only, we decided to add something else, which – we believe – is going to be interesting for all our readers.

As we are talking about the kitchen, it is time to introduce one of the most famous Italian recipes. Have a guess...

The world-renowned **pasta alla carbonara**, of course!

We will add the *real* recipe of this tasty dish in Italian first, followed by its translation in English. Our goal is not only to give you an idea of what to cook for dinner, but also to introduce some useful vocabulary that is definitely going to come in handy if you like cooking or if you are interested in Italian recipes.

We have highlighted the most common verbs that can be found in Italian recipes. We believe that you are going to be surprised to discover how simple – yet delicious – this **ricetta** is!

We hope that you are not too hungry because this recipe will definitely make you salivate.

 Pasta alla carbonara

Ingredienti:

- Pasta (spaghetti)
- Pepe nero q.b.
- Pecorino (50g)
- Tuorli d'uova (6)
- Guanciale (150g)

Per preparare la pasta alla carbonara mettete una pentola sul fuoco. Mentre aspettate, tagliate il guanciale a strisce spesse circa 1cm.

Mettete i pezzetti di guanciale in una padella antiaderente e rosolate per circa 10 minuti. Il guanciale deve diventare croccante, ma non nero.

Quando l'acqua bolle, versate gli spaghetti e aggiungete un pizzico di sale grosso. Poi versate i tuorli d'uovo in una ciotola. Aggiungete il pecorino e anche il pepe nero. Mescolate il composto fino a ottenere una crema omogenea.

Quando il guanciale è pronto, mettetelo in una piccola ciotola. Scolate la pasta al dente e, nella padella, versate anche il composto con uova e pecorino, mescolando velocemente. Potete anche aggiungere un po' di acqua di cottura della pasta per rendere la pasta più cremosa.

Aggiungete il guanciale e mescolate ancora una volta. Servite aggiungendo un po' di pecorino e un pizzico di pepe.

Ingredients:

- *Pasta (spaghetti)*
- *Black pepper to taste*
- *Pecorino cheese 50g*
- *Egg yolks (6)*
- *Guanciale 150g*

To prepare the pasta alla carbonara, put a pot of water on the stove. While you wait for the water to boil, cut the guanciale into strips about 1/2" thick.

Put the guanciale strips into a non-stick pan and cook for about 10 minutes. The guanciale should become crispy, but not burned.

When the water is boiling, pour in the spaghetti and add a pinch of coarse salt. Then put the yolks into a bowl. Add Pecorino cheese and black pepper. Stir the mixture until you get a smooth cream.

When the guanciale is ready, put it in a small bowl. Drain the pasta al dente and add it to the pan, together with the mixture of yolks and pecorino cheese. Stir quickly. You can also add a bit of cooking water to make the dish creamier.

Add the crispy strips of guanciale and stir one more time. Add some Pecorino cheese and black pepper on top and serve.

Well, before finishing this (tasty) chapter, there is just one more thing to say:

Buon appetito! *Enjoy your meal!*

📝 EXERCISES II

1) **Aggiungi i nomi degli oggetti all'immagine.** *Add the Italian words for the items shown in the image below.*

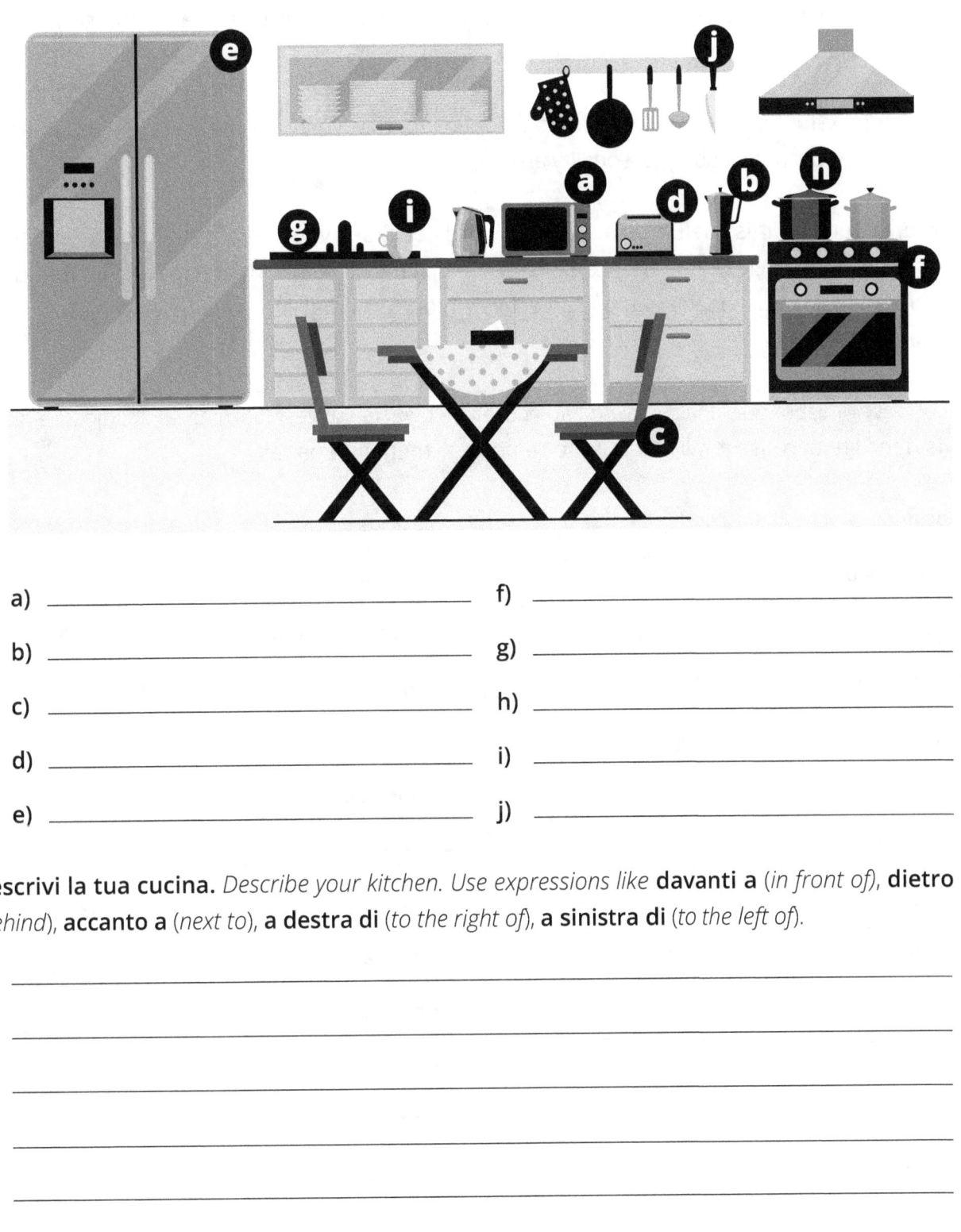

a) _____   f) _____

b) _____   g) _____

c) _____   h) _____

d) _____   i) _____

e) _____   j) _____

2) **Descrivi la tua cucina.** *Describe your kitchen. Use expressions like* **davanti a** *(in front of),* **dietro** *(behind),* **accanto a** *(next to),* **a destra di** *(to the right of),* **a sinistra di** *(to the left of).*

_____

_____

_____

_____

_____

CHAPTER 3
PERSONALITY

With this chapter, you are going to learn how to describe your personality and someone else's. Why should you learn this kind of vocabulary, though?

Well, for example, if you are planning on working in Italy, you will probably have job interviews to attend, so questions about personality are quite common.

Also, in general, it is useful to know these words because you can often find them in movies, TV series, books, articles... And they can also come in handy if you want to make Italian friends! Not to mention that we use many of these adjectives in our everyday life, even when they are not strictly related to someone's personality.

Look at our list of personality-related adjectives below. We suggest learning each adjective along with its opposite because it will be easier to remember them as a pair.

buono	*good*	**cattivo**	*bad/mean*
simpatico	*friendly*	**antipatico**	*unpleasant*
generoso	*generous*	**taccagno/tirchio**	*stingy*
paziente	*patient*	**impaziente**	*impatient*
felice	*happy*	**triste**	*sad*
educato	*polite*	**maleducato**	*rude*
espansivo	*expansive*	**riservato**	*reserved*
estroverso	*outgoing*	**timido**	*shy*
altruista	*altruistic*	**egoista**	*selfish*
ottimista	*optimistic*	**pessimista**	*pessimistic*
coraggioso	*brave*	**codardo**	*coward*
attivo	*active*	**pigro**	*lazy*
riflessivo	*reflective*	**impulsivo**	*impulsive*

affidabile	*reliable*	**inaffidabile**	*unreliable*
sincero/onesto	*sincere/honest*	**bugiardo**	*liar*
sicuro di sé	*confident*	**insicuro**	*insecure*
taciturno	*reserved*	**chiacchierone**	*chatty*
sensibile	*sensitive*	**insensibile**	*insensitive*

Of course, it is hard – if not impossible – to include all the personality-related adjectives in a short list, but we believe that the ones above are the most used.

Also, we remind you that the adjectives in our list are in their masculine singular form. Whenever you use them, you will have to change them according to the gender and number of the person to whom you are referring – as usual.

Now, moving on to the fun part of this chapter. In the list below, you will find some interesting Italian expressions referring to someone's personality, which are commonly used by native speakers.

- **avere un caratteraccio** *to have a temper*

False friend alert! The Italian word **carattere** does not mean *character* – which is translated as **personaggio**. Just like its synonym **personalità**, it means *personality*. Also, the suffix **-accio** is pejorative. So **carattere+accio** is a word+suffix mix we use to refer to a bad temper.

- **avere i piedi per terra** *to be down-to-earth*

Literally translated as *to have the feet on the ground*, this is a very common expression to describe a humble person.

- **essere una vipera** *to be mean*

This expression is quite self-explanatory. C'mon, is there anything meaner than a viper?

- **essere fuori dagli schemi** *to be unconventional*

This expression is literally translated as *to be out of the schemes*, meaning that someone does not follow them, and acts in a different way. Please note that this expression is not necessarily considered a negative one!

- **essere in gamba** — *to be capable/smart*

Would you be able to understand the real meaning of this expression if you translated it literally – *to be in leg*?!

- **essere furbo come una volpe** — *to be as sly as a fox*

An easy one with an equivalent translation in English!

- **essere una persona di sani principi** — *to be someone with good (moral) values*

Pronunciation alert! How would you read the word **principi**? *preen-chi-pee,* right? But where would you put the stress? If you remember, Italian words can only have an accent on the last letter. However, if we want to write the proper pronunciation of this noun, we could write *preen-chì-pee*, meaning that the stress would be on the second *i*.

Why is it so important, though? Because the very same word exists with different stress, and a very different meaning. In fact, the Italian word **prìncipi** – once again, the accent above the first *i* is an "imaginary" one, only to guide you with the pronunciation – means *princes*!

EXERCISES III

1) **Aggiungi le traduzioni mancanti.** *Add the missing translations of the opposites in the table below.*

coraggioso	
	cattivo
	timido
sensibile	
egoista	
	taciturno
felice	
bugiardo	
	antipatico

2) **Descrivi la tua personalità!** *Now describe your own personality, or someone else's. Try to be brutally honest when it comes to strengths and weaknesses – nnot only is no one perfect, but most importantly, no one else is going to read this!*

CHAPTER 4
FUTURE PERFECT

One chapter about vocabulary, one chapter about grammar, **e così via...** – *and so on.*

After learning some useful personality-related vocabulary, it is time to focus on grammar one more time, but we promise that this chapter is not going to be a long one!

The future tense, again?

Well, yes. If you think about it, there is another future tense in English as well, and one that we use quite frequently. Known as *future perfect*, this tense is used when we want to talk about an action/event that will be completed at a certain point in the future, before another action in the future.

This is how we form this tense in English:

Subject + will have (invariable) + past participle of the main verb

The good news is that there is an Italian tense that strictly corresponds to the English *future perfect*, and it is the so-called **futuro anteriore**. Basically, whenever you use that tense in English, you will have to use the **futuro anteriore** in Italian.

Now, let's see how we form it in Italian:

(soggetto) + ausiliare essere/avere al futuro + participio passato

Its structure is not that different from that of the future perfect, right? The only difference is that you will have to choose between *to be* and *to have* as the auxiliary verb. Also, the same auxiliary verb needs to be conjugated in the future tense.

As previously discussed in our Italian Made Easy Level 1 workbook, we told you that it was worth a read! You will pick **avere** if the main verb – the one in the past participle – is a transitive one, and **essere** if it is an intransitive verb.

Should we review the definition of transitive and intransitive verbs?

Yeah, let's quickly do it before moving forward. Reviewing is always a good thing, especially with foreign languages!

In short, a transitive verb is a verb requiring an *object* to make sense. If we take the verb *to do* as an example, would it make sense if we do not add a direct object?

In fact, if we just say *I do*, the spontaneous question that someone would ask is: *What?* Well, to be honest, the only scenario where a short sentence like that one would make sense on its own is when someone is at the altar getting married! In fact, the verb *to do* is a transitive one, meaning that it needs a direct object – for example, *I do my homework*.

Intransitive verbs are the opposite. They do *not* need a direct object to make sense. We can add a full stop right after the verb and the sentence would be complete and make perfect sense. Sometimes these verbs can be followed by other words, for example adverbs, but not by direct objects for sure.

An example of a sentence with an intransitive verb can be *They go to the gym on Saturdays*. Besides congratulating them on being so motivated, you can see that the main verb – *to go* – is not transitive because you cannot answer the questions *What?* or *Who?*

On the other hand, the verb can answer the question *Where?* And that is a question for an intransitive verb.

Okay, now that we have reviewed the definition of transitive and intransitive verbs, we need to remind you that if your verb is intransitive and requires *to be* as the auxiliary, you must adapt the past participle according to the gender and number of the subject.

Examples:

- **Tra un mese avranno finito gli studi.**
  They will have finished their studies in a month.
- **L'anno prossimo saremo molto impegnati.**
  Next year we will be very busy.

In order to help you build your first sentences with the future perfect, let's look at a couple of examples of verbs conjugated in this tense, one requiring the auxiliary *to have*, and the other one with *to be*.

soggetto	prendere *to take*	partire *to leave*
io	avrò preso	sarò partito/a
tu	avrai preso	sarai partito/a
lui/lei/Lei	avrà preso	sarà partito/a
noi	avremo preso	saremo partiti/e
voi	avrete preso	sarete partiti/e
loro	avranno preso	saranno partiti/e

Please note that the verb **prendere** has an irregular past participle – **preso**. Do not hesitate to look at our list of irregular past participles at the end of the workbook whenever you have a doubt. Even though it is not a comprehensive list, it includes the most common irregular past participles.

Just like with the **passato prossimo**, the past participle never changes when we use *to have* as the auxiliary. The only verb that changes is the auxiliary itself, which needs to be conjugated in the simple future.

The example requiring *to be* as the auxiliary is the verb **partire**. In this instance, the past participle will change according to the subject. This is why there are four options for the past participle, two for the singular and two for the plural – one masculine and one feminine.

Compared to the English future perfect, there may be one little exception regarding the use of this tense in Italian. Sometimes, the future perfect is also used to make assumptions or hypotheses about something that happened in the past. We know... It is weird indeed.

For the same kind of situation, we would use the construction "must have..." in English. Please look at the examples below.

Examples:

- **Dove sono?**
  Avranno preso il bus.
  Where are they?
  They must have taken the bus.

- **Si sarà dimenticato il portafoglio a casa.**
  He must have forgotten his wallet at home.

EXERCISES IV

1) **Coniuga i seguenti verbi al futuro anteriore.** *Conjugate the verbs in the table below in the future perfect. Beware! There may be some irregular ones.*

soggetto	lavare to wash	scrivere to write	essere to be
io			
tu			
lui/lei/Lei			
noi			
voi			
loro			

2) **Ascolta l'audio.** *Listen to the audio file and add the missing words in the text.*

Tra cinque anni _____ sicuramente un lavoro che _____!

_____ per diventare un ingegnere, e _____ un mese fa.

Spero di _____ dei colleghi simpatici e _____

e di _____ un appartamento accogliente. Ah, tra cinque anni, Io e la mia

compagna _____ genitori!

Translation

In five years, I will have found a job that I like for sure! I studied to become an engineer, and I graduated a month ago. I hope to meet friendly and smart colleagues and to rent a cozy apartment. Ah! In five years, my girlfriend and I will have become parents!

CHAPTER 5
THE HUMAN BODY, PT. 1

You know what is coming, right?

After a grammar chapter, it is time to discover a new vocabulary topic! And this time we will start focusing on the *human body* – **il corpo umano**.

You already know why it is important to know the vocabulary related to body parts, and not only in case something unfortunate happens while you are in Italy – though we hope that you will never need these words for this reason!

However, **prevenire è sempre meglio che curare** – *better safe than sorry* – and this is why we decided to introduce this topic in our second workbook on the Italian language.

With this first chapter, we are going to introduce the vocabulary related to the upper part of the body only, as there is a lot to say and we do not want to **mettere troppa carne sul fuoco** – literally, *to put too much meat on the stove*, meaning adding too much information, all at once.

Let's start with the *head* – **la testa**:

faccia/viso	*face*	**lingua**	*tongue*
capelli	*hair*	**naso**	*nose*
occhio	*eye*	**narici**	*nostrils*
ciglia	*eyelashes*	**orecchio**	*ear*
sopracciglia	*eyebrows*	**mento**	*chin*
guance	*cheeks*	**barba**	*beard*
bocca	*mouth*	**baffi**	*moustache*
labbra	*lips*	**fronte**	*forehead*
denti	*teeth*	**tempie**	*temples*
gengive	*gums*	**lentiggini**	*freckles*

A few things to highlight regarding some of the words above:

- Unlike English, the word **capelli** is plural. Its singular form does exist – **capello** – but it is not frequently used as it refers to just one of your hairs. Also, beware! *Body hair* is a completely different word in Italian, and it is **peli**.

- One last thing: try not to mistake **capelli** with **cappelli**. We know that it is just a matter of an extra *p*, but if you say *cappelli*, you are now talking about *hats*!

- **Ciglia, sopracciglia, labbra,** and **orecchie** behave in a very weird way. When plural, they are feminine. However, when they are in their singular form, they become masculine! **Un ciglio, un sopracciglio, un labbro, un orecchio**.

- Fun fact: the word **sopracciglia** literally means *above the eyelashes*, and we guess that it makes sense, doesn't it?

- Unlike English, the singular form of *teeth* – **denti** – is a very regular one, **dente.**

- Yeah... the Italian word **lingua** can mean both *tongue* and *language* – **la lingua italiana**.

Should we go a bit lower now? Let's take a look at the vocabulary associated with the body from the neck to the hips.

collo	*neck*	**avambraccio**	*forearm*
spalla	*shoulder*	**polso**	*wrist*
clavicola	*collarbone*	**mano**	*hand*
scapola	*shoulder blade*	**pollice**	*thumb*
schiena	*back*	**dita**	*fingers*
bassa schiena	*lower back*	**unghia**	*nail*
petto	*chest*	**stomaco**	*stomach*
seno	*breast*	**costole**	*ribs*
ascella	*armpit*	**pancia**	*belly*
braccio	*arm*	**ombelico**	*navel*
gomito	*elbow*	**fianchi**	*hips*

Once again, take a look at these interesting facts about the words above:

- The Italian word **braccio** is another weird one with a masculine singular form and a feminine plural one – **le braccia**. The same applies to **il dito/le dita** – *finger/fingers*.

- Just a memo: the Italian combination of letters *schi* – as in **schiena** – must be read as *ski*.

- There is an Italian expression corresponding to the English *elbow grease* to refer to a situation requiring a big physical effort – **olio di gomito**!

One last important thing. What would you say in Italian if something hurts?

The Italian expressions you need to use to say something hurts are **mi fa male...** or **mi fanno male**. These expressions are followed by the name of the body part that hurts. You will need to use the first one for singular nouns – for example, **mi fa male la pancia** – and the second one for plural nouns – as in **mi fanno male le costole**. We hope that you will not need to say them, though!

📝 EXERCISES V

1) **Aggiungi i nomi delle parti del corpo.** *Add the names of the following body parts in Italian.*

2) **Descrivi il tuo viso!** *Write a short description of your face. Use the verb to have and useful adjectives like* piccolo *or* grande *and the colors too.*

_____
_____
_____
_____
_____
_____
_____

EXTRA
ITALIAN SONGS

As we have just finished our second unit, you knew that this section was coming...

La nostra seconda canzone italiana! *Our second Italian song!*

You are probably wondering which song we have picked this time... The song we chose for our new extra section is **Meraviglioso**, which is a song with truly **meraviglioso** – *wonderful* – lyrics originally sung by **Domenico Modugno** in 1968 and then reinterpreted by the Italian band **Negramaro** in 2008.

Once again, do not hesitate to listen to the song while reading its lyrics. You can also listen to both versions and decide which one you like the most!

 Meraviglioso (Domenico Modugno)

È vero
It is true

Credetemi è accaduto
Believe me, it happened

Di notte su di un ponte
At night, on a bridge

Guardando l'acqua scura
Staring at the dark water

Con la dannata voglia
With the damn desire

Di fare un tuffo giù
Of jumping off

D'un tratto
All of a sudden

Qualcuno alle mie spalle
Someone behind me

Forse un angelo
Maybe an angel

Vestito da passante
Disguised as a passerby

Mi portò via dicendomi
Took me away telling me

Così...
These words...

Meraviglioso
Wonderful

Ma come non ti accorgi
How come you do not realize

Di quanto il mondo sia
How the world is

Meraviglioso
Wonderful

Meraviglioso
Wonderful

Perfino il tuo dolore
Even your pain

Potrà guarire poi
Will be able to heal

Meraviglioso
Wonderful

Ma guarda intorno a te
Look around you

Che doni ti hanno fatto
At the gifts you have been given

Ti hanno inventato
For you, they created

Il mare
The sea

Tu dici non ho niente
You say 'I have nothing'

Ti sembra niente il sole?
Do you feel like the sun is nothing?

La vita...
Life...

L'amore...
Love...

Meraviglioso
Wonderful

Il bene di una donna
The love of a woman

Che ama solo te
Who loves you only

Meraviglioso
Wonderful

La luce di un mattino
The morning light

L'abbraccio di un amico
A friend's hug

Il viso di un bambino
A child's face

Meraviglioso
Wonderful

Ma guarda intorno a te
Look around you

Che doni ti hanno fatto
At the gifts you have been given

Ti hanno inventato
For you, they created

Il mare
The sea

Tu dici non ho niente
You say 'I have nothing'

Ti sembra niente il sole?
Do you feel like the sun is nothing?

La vita...
Life...

L'amore...
Love...

Meraviglioso...
Wonderful

Il bene di una donna
The love of a woman

Che ama solo te
loves only you

La notte era finita
The night was over

E ti sentivo ancora
And I could still feel you

Sapore della vita
Flavor of life

Meraviglioso...
Wonderful...

Well, this song truly is **un'ode alla vita** – *an ode to life*. And we hope you liked it as much as we do.

It tells us a story about a man who believes to have nothing in his life until someone else reminds him of all the precious things he has been given – **il mare, il sole, la vita, l'amore...**

As usual, let's now focus on a few interesting vocabulary points:

credetemi: the pronoun is attached to the conjugated verb in the imperative tense – we'll come back to this later. **Credete+mi,** *believe me!*

Example:

- **Ho studiato tutto il giorno. Credetemi!** *I studied all day. Believe me!*

è accaduto: simple past of the verb *to happen,* which in Italian has two possible translations – **accadere,** as in the song lyrics, and **succedere**. However, the second one is more common than the first one, which is not used much in daily conversations and nowadays sounds a bit more "poetic." Please note that the verb **succedere** has an irregular past participle – **successo**. By the way, the same word could also mean *success.*

ma come: when you see a question starting with these two words, you would generally translate it as *How come...?*

Example:

- **Non vieni più? Ma come?** *You are not coming anymore? How come?*

sia: for now, let's not worry too much about this verb. Why? Because it is the verb *to be,* a verb with which you are now very familiar, but conjugated in a mood that we have not introduced yet – **il congiuntivo**, *the subjunctive tense*. Please note that, if you ever come across the words **sia... sia...** within the same sentence, it is not the repetition of the same verb, but rather the Italian for *both... and...*

poi: probably the most common word to say *then*. Do not be tempted to say **dopo** all the time, because its most appropriate translation is *after*.

doni: a more poetic version of the more common noun **regali** – *gifts*.

il bene di una donna: these few words allow us to introduce an interesting difference between English and Italian when it comes to expressing your feelings toward another person.

In fact, in Italian, there are two main expressions: **ti voglio bene** and **ti amo**. In English, both would be translated as *I love you*. However, they have two very different meanings in Italian!

The first expression could be literally translated as *I want good things for you*, hence *I care about you*.

This is the kind of thing you would say to a friend, to a family member, or even to your partner at the beginning of a relationship, when your feelings are starting to grow.

On the other hand, **ti amo** refers to a much deeper, romantic love. Whenever you say **ti amo** to someone, it means that you have strong, deep feelings for them. The two expressions represent the natural evolution of a relationship: at the beginning **vuoi bene a quella persona**, then – after some time – **la ami.**

In short, it would be weird if someone says **ti amo** to a friend, and it would be equally weird if someone said "just" **ti voglio bene** to their husband/wife! Then, of course, every person – and relationship – is different and everyone is completely entitled to express their feelings however they want – so please consider this short paragraph as a very generic explanation of an Italian custom when it comes to relationships.

UNIT 3
RUNNING TOWARD FLUENCY

CHAPTER 1
DEMONSTRATIVE ADJECTIVES

Demonstrative... What?

Even though you may not be familiar with their definition, you know what we are talking about for sure! Demonstrative adjectives are those adjectives we use to point at an object, a person, an animal, etc.

In English, we have two demonstrative adjectives: *this* and *that*, whose plural forms are *these* and *those*, respectively.

Good news! In Italian, it is the same thing. The two demonstrative adjectives – **gli aggettivi dimostrativi** – are **questo** and **quello**. On the other hand, Italian adjectives, articles etc. need to match the gender and number of the noun to which they refer, and the same applies to demonstrative adjectives, too.

Here are the different forms of the Italian demonstrative adjectives:

masculine singular	feminine singular	masculine plural	feminine plural
questo quest'	questa quest'	questi	queste
quello quel quell'	quella quell'	quegli quei	quelle

Before moving forward with our explanation, let's talk about the difference between **questo/quello**. The first one corresponds to *this* and the second one to *that*. There is nothing more to say about it.

Another thing you should know is that there is a third demonstrative adjective in Italian, which is kind of a synonym of **quello** – **codesto/a/i/e**. However, we decided not to mention it right away because it is very unlikely that you are going to come across it, as it is no longer used. You may find it in books, but Italians no longer use it in their everyday life.

The only exception could be represented by the people living in Tuscany, who may still use that demonstrative adjective even if it is on the verge of extinction there as well.

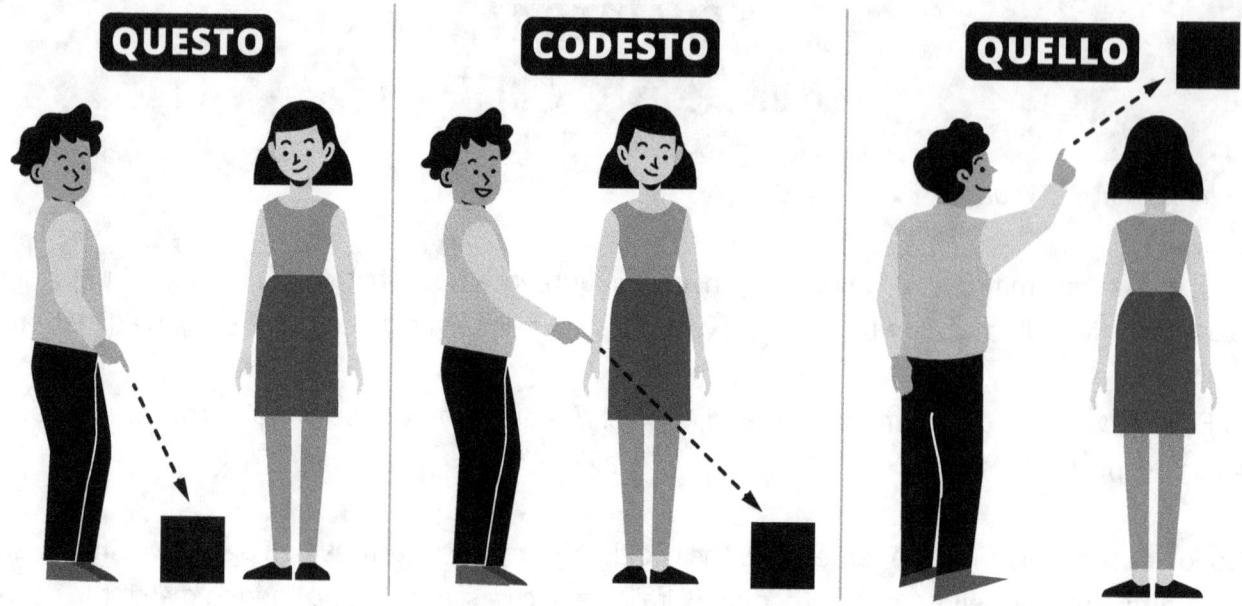

Now, let's discuss the different forms of the Italian demonstrative adjectives.

You may have noticed **quest'** – with that little apostrophe: we use it whenever the following noun begins with a vowel.

Examples:

- **Quest'uomo è mio zio.** *This man is my uncle.*
- **Quest'opera è molto moderna.** *This artwork is very modern.*

Now let's look at the masculine singular forms of *that*: **quello, quel,** and **quell'**. To better understand them, think about the Italian definite articles. We use **quel** for most masculine nouns beginning with a consonant – the nouns requiring **il** as definite article – and **quello** for all those nouns which would require **lo** as definite article – so the nouns beginning with *s+consonant, gn, ps, pn, x, y, z...* On the other hand, **quell'** is used for masculine and feminine nouns beginning with a vowel.

Examples:

- **Quello zaino è mio.** *That backpack is mine.*
- **Quel cane corre nel parco.** *That dog runs in the park.*
- **Quell'aereo sta volando basso.** *That plane is flying low.*

Quegli is the plural of **quello,** and **quei** is the plural of **quel**. For plural masculine nouns starting with a vowel, we will use **quegli** as well. To explain it better, we will use the same sentences again, but in their plural form.

Examples:

- **Quegli zaini sono miei.** — *Those backpacks are mine.*
- **Quei cani corrono nel parco.** — *Those dogs run in the park.*
- **Quegli aerei stanno volando basso.** — *Those planes are flying low.*

EXERCISES I

1) **Completa la tabella.** *Complete the table below with the different forms of the Italian demonstrative adjectives. Please write all the possibilities.*

masculine singular	feminine singular	masculine plural	feminine plural

2) **Completa le seguenti frasi.** *Complete the sentences below with the correct form of demonstrative adjective.*

   a) Che cos'è _____ caos?
   What is this chaos?

   b) _____ macchina laggiù è molto costosa.
   That car over there is very expensive.

   c) I nostri figli sono _____ ragazzi con la maglietta blu.
   Our sons are those guys with a blue t-shirt.

   d) _____ anno andranno negli Stati Uniti.
   This year they will go to the United States.

   e) Adoro _____ casette! Spero di comprarne una.
   I love these little houses! I hope to buy one.

   f) _____ videogioco gli è piaciuto molto.
   He liked that videogame a lot.

   g) _____ uffici sono grandi, ma non sono in centro.
   Those offices are big, but they are not in the city center.

CHAPTER 2
THE HOUSE, PT. 3

In Unit 2, we talked about the vocabulary related to the kitchen, and it is now time to move forward and explore another room. Specifically, one of the most important ones: *the bedroom* – **la camera da letto**.

If you think about it, it is probably the room where we spend most of our time. This is why it is important to learn the vocabulary associated with it. In fact, you will need it if you live in Italy already, and also if you are planning to rent/buy a property there and need to discuss some of the items in it. For example, if you have booked a hotel room, you might need to know these words if you want to ask for something at the front desk.

Let's get started, then. In the list below, you will find the translations of the most common items that can be found in a bedroom and a few useful adjectives.

letto	*bed*	**lampadario**	*ceiling light*
letto singolo	*single bed*	**scrivania**	*desk*
letto matrimoniale	*double bed*	**sedia**	*chair*
letto alla francese	*French bed*	**tappeto**	*carpet*
letto a castello	*bunk bed*	**finestra**	*window*
materasso	*mattress*	**tende**	*curtains*
lenzuola	*sheets*	**persiana**	*shutter*
coperta	*blanket*	**orologio**	*clock*
trapunta	*duvet*	**armadio**	*wardrobe*
cuscino	*pillow*	**cabina armadio**	*walk-in closet*
morbido	*soft*	**mensola**	*shelf*
duro	*hard*	**libreria**	*bookshelf*
cotone	*cotton*	**cornice**	*frame*
flanella	*flannel*	**quadro**	*painting*
seta	*silk*	**pavimento**	*floor*
comodino	*nightstand*	**soffitto**	*ceiling*
lampada/abat-jour	*bedside lamp*		

Of course, the list above is not comprehensive, as there may be tons of different things in someone's bedroom. However, those are probably the most common and useful words associated with bedrooms in general.

Now, let's take a closer look at some interesting facts about some of the words mentioned above:

- The Italian word for *double bed* is **letto matrimoniale,** which is literally translated as *matrimonial bed!* **Letto doppio,** instead, generally refers to a double pull-out bed, meaning that there is a spare bed below a single one, and it can be pulled out when necessary.

- *Sheets* is another of those weird Italian words with a masculine singular form – **il lenzuolo** – and a feminine plural form – **le lenzuola** – as we have already seen for some body parts in the previous unit.

- When it comes to talking about materials in Italian, the preposition you should use is **di. Example**: **Ho le lenzuola di cotone**, *I have cotton sheets*.

- *False friend alert!* **Libreria** is a false friend as it does not mean *library* – **biblioteca** – but rather *bookshelf* or *bookshop*.

- **Camera da letto** usually refers to a bedroom for adults. In fact, the most common word used for a child's bedroom is **cameretta**. The suffix *-etta* is a diminutive one, so **cameretta** literally means *little bedroom*. Please note that the adjective *little* does not apply to the size of the bedroom itself, but to the size of their owners!

- In a house/apartment, there may also be a **camera per gli ospiti** – *a guest room*. Even though the Italian word is very similar to the English *hospital*, do not worry. **Ospiti** means *guests*, and *guests* only!

EXERCISES II

1) **Scrivi il nome degli oggetti nella camera da letto.** *Write the Italian names of the items in the bedroom shown below.*

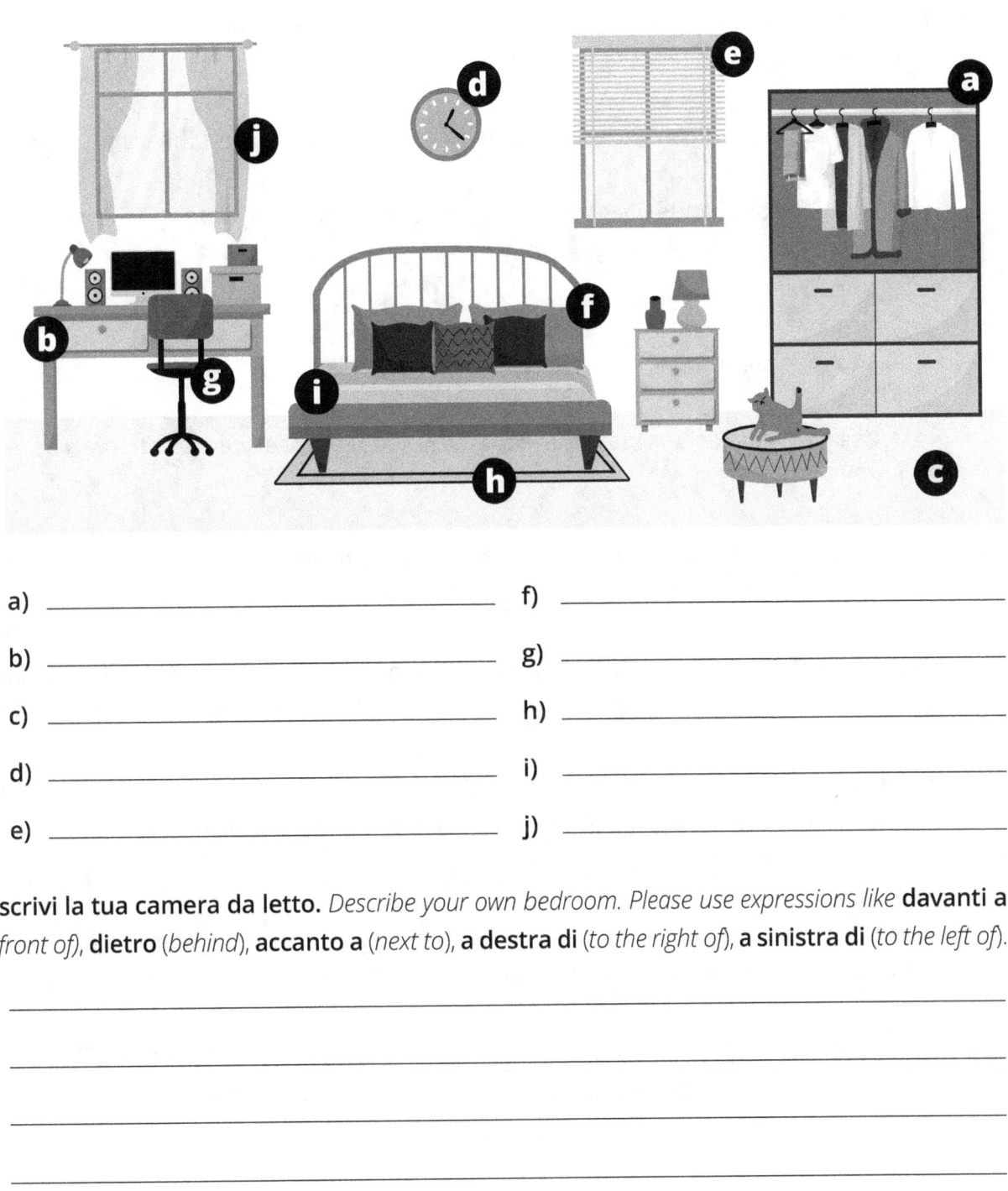

a) _____ f) _____

b) _____ g) _____

c) _____ h) _____

d) _____ i) _____

e) _____ j) _____

2) **Descrivi la tua camera da letto.** *Describe your own bedroom. Please use expressions like* **davanti a** *(in front of),* **dietro** *(behind),* **accanto a** *(next to),* **a destra di** *(to the right of),* **a sinistra di** *(to the left of).*

_____

_____

_____

_____

_____

CHAPTER 3
THE IMPERATIVE MOOD

Learn the verb conjugation in Italian! Well, that was a good example of imperative mood in English, a tense we use for direct commands and requests. However, it is important to remember that using the imperative mood does not necessarily mean being rude.

In fact, there are different situations requiring the use of this mood. Look at the short summary below:

- Positive commands: *Please open the window; clean your room if you have time today; save your files on your computer as well;* etc.

- Negative commands: *Do not smoke in restaurants; do not be late for your first day at work; please do not send me emails while I am on holiday;* etc.

- Call to action: *Let's invite our friends over; let's go to the cinema with the kids; let's cook lunch together;* etc.

As you can see, in English, whenever we use the imperative mood, we do not always need a subject pronoun. In general, the sentence will start with an invariable verb.

In Italian, it is a little bit different. Before delving into the differences between the two languages, it is important to highlight that in Italian we use this mood in the same situations/contexts as in English.

On the other hand, in Italian, your sentence will not start with an invariable verb because you will have to conjugate the verb itself. The good news is that you already know the verb conjugation, because the verb will be conjugated in the present tense!

Also, compared to the "typical" verb conjugation in the present tense, there are fewer possibilities when you use the imperative mood that we are going to explain right away.

First option: You can conjugate the verb according to the subject pronoun *you*, singular – **tu**. **Exception alert!** If you want to conjugate a verb belonging to the **-are** group, the verb ending will not be **-i** – as in the simple present – but **-a**.

Examples:

- **Prendi i bicchieri!** *Take the glasses!*

    In this instance, the conjugated verb is just like the simple present – **tu prendi** – as it is a verb belonging to the **-ere** group – **prendere**.

- **Mangia le verdure!** *Eat your vegetables!*

    Here, you can see that the conjugated verb in the imperative mood does not correspond to the conjugated verb in the simple present – which would be **tu mangi** – because **mangiare** is a verb belonging to the **-are** group.

Second option: You can conjugate the verb according to the subject pronoun *she* – **Lei** – to use the courtesy form. You probably know it already because it is a topic we discussed in the first workbook. But in Italian you need to use the courtesy form when talking with someone you do not know, someone who is older than you, or is in a higher position. In all these instances, you need to use **Lei** as subject pronoun and conjugate the verb accordingly, no matter the gender of the person to whom you are talking.

With the imperative mood, though, the tense to use is the *present subjunctive* – **il congiuntivo presente.** The same applies to the subject pronoun *they* – **loro**. However, we will not introduce this mood in this workbook because it is one of the most advanced grammar topics.

For now, just keep this information in mind, and if possible, try to avoid the imperative mood in the 3rd person singular or plural when speaking in Italian! ;)

Third option: You can conjugate the verb according to the subject pronoun *we* – **noi** – as you do in the present tense. In English, this is the equivalent of *Let's*.

Example:

- **Studiamo questo libro fantastico di italiano!** *Let's study this amazing Italian workbook!*

Fourth option: Finally, we can conjugate the verb according to the subject pronoun *you* plural – **voi** – in the present tense.

Example:

- **Andate a scuola o farete tardi!** *Go to school or you will be late!*

Now that we have explained the different available options for the verb conjugation in the imperative mood, let's look – **diamo un'occhiata** – at a few examples in the table below.

soggetto	**studiare** *to study*	**leggere** *to read*	**dormire** *to sleep*
tu	studia!	leggi!	dormi!
Lei	studi!	legga!	dorma!
noi	studiamo!	leggiamo!	dormiamo!
voi	studiate!	leggete!	dormite!
loro	studino!	leggano!	dormano!

When it comes to negative commands, their construction is very easy: you will need to add a **non** in front of the verb, just as you do with the present tense.

Important! In negative sentences requiring the imperative mood, the verb must be used in its infinitive form when the subject pronoun is *you*, singular, but you will have to conjugate it with all the other subject pronouns.

Examples:

- Non <u>chiamare</u> l'ufficio!   *Don't call the office!*
- Non <u>tornate</u> tardi stasera.   *Don't come home late tonight.*

And what if we want to conjugate a reflexive verb in the imperative mood?

Well, in this instance, the reflexive pronoun will be attached at the end of the verb – weird, right?

Let's make it clearer with an example. **Ti vesti elegante** is an example of sentence with a reflexive verb conjugated in the present tense whose infinitive is **vestirsi**. It means *you get dressed up*. The same sentence in the imperative mood would be **vestiti elegante!** You can see how the reflexive pronoun **ti** is not before the verb itself but is now attached to the conjugated verb **vesti**.

However, the rule above does not apply when we use the imperative mood with the subject pronouns **Lei** and **loro,** as we must use the verb conjugated in the present subjunctive tense, as already mentioned.

To finish this chapter and show you how the conjugation of a reflexive verb looks, we added a couple of examples in the table below. You will immediately notice the different position of the pronouns for **Lei** and **loro**.

soggetto	alzarsi *to get up*	prepararsi *to get ready*
tu	alzati!	preparati!
Lei	si alzi!	si prepari!
noi	alziamoci!	prepariamoci!
voi	alzatevi!	preparatevi!
loro	si alzino!	si preparino!

EXERCISES III

1) **Scrivi la coniugazione dei verbi all'imperativo.** *Write the conjugation of the following verbs in the imperative mood.*

soggetto	guardare *to watch*	pentirsi *to regret*	scrivere *to write*
tu			
Lei	guardi!	si penta!	scriva!
noi			
voi			
loro	guardino!	si pentano!	scrivano!

2) **Scrivi l'ordine/la richiesta corrispondente alla situazione.** *Write the command/ request according to the context using the imperative mood. Beware! There may be reflexive verbs, too.*

Example: He is at home   ......non fumare...... (fumare, to smoke)

a) He is in the classroom   _____ (correre, to run)

b) We are at the restaurant   _____ (mangiare, to eat)

c) You have an exam   _____ (studiare, tu, to study)

d) He is late   _____ (muoversi, to hurry)

e) You are hungry   _____ (cucinare, voi, to cook)

f) He is angry   _____ (calmarsi, to calm down)

CHAPTER 4
COMPUTING AND IT

Maybe you are an IT lover or professional, or perhaps you are not into technology at all, and a pen and paper are still your best friends. In any case, nowadays technology is all around us, and this is why it is important to know some useful vocabulary related to the digital world.

With this chapter, we won't really get into details, but we will rather focus on three macro-fields within this world, which we believe are also the most useful/common ones: *mobile devices, computers and surfing the Internet, and social media* – **cellulari, computer e navigazione su internet, e social network.**

In fact, in one way or another, most people must deal with them on a daily basis. And you can imagine that, if you are in a foreign country, and your computer does not work, it is important to know how to describe that problem. Or maybe you want to buy a new phone. In that case, you will have to explain what you are looking for, or understand what the salesperson is telling you.

Good news! When it comes to technology, the Italian language has adopted many English words. A relevant thing to highlight: generally speaking, all English words used in Italian are masculine, and, more important, they are <u>invariable</u>, meaning that their singular form is just like the plural one. For example, in Italian you will say **un computer, due computer** – *one computer, two computers*.

Now, let's start with some vocabulary associated with **i cellulari,** shall we?

schermo	*screen*	**messaggi**	*texts*
cover (feminine)	*cover*	**chiamate**	*calls*
fotocamera	*camera*	**rubrica/contatti**	*contacts*
flash	*flash*	**audio/video**	*audio/video*
zoom	*zoom*	**calendario**	*calendar*
batteria	*battery*	**impostazioni**	*settings*
risparmio energetico	*low power mode*	**mappe**	*maps*
caricabatteria	*charger*	**note**	*notes*
silenzioso	*silent mode*	**applicazione/app**	*app*
modalità aereo	*airplane mode*		

As you can see, most of the words above are English ones, or they are quite similar to their corresponding English translations.

If you want to learn more about mobile-related vocabulary, our advice is to change the language of your personal devices. Try to switch it to Italian. You will see that, at first, it may be a little difficult to find what you are seeking, but you will soon get used to it and, most importantly, this is how you will learn a lot of new words!

Now let's move on to **i computer e la navigazione su internet**. However, we will not repeat the words already mentioned in the previous section, such as *screen, battery*, etc. Let's go!

computer fisso	*PC*	**cronologia**	*history*
computer portatile	*laptop*	**sito (web)**	*website*
tablet	*tablet*	**connessione**	*connection*
accendere	*to switch on*	**cliccare**	*to click*
spegnere	*to switch off*	**cancellare**	*to delete*
programmi/software	*software*	**selezionare**	*to select*
Wi-Fi	*Wi-Fi*	**sottolineare**	*to underline*
tastiera	*keyboard*	**invio**	*enter*
tasto	*key*	**grassetto**	*bold*
mouse	*mouse*	**corsivo**	*italic*
password	*password*	**file**	*file*
nome utente	*username*	**cartella**	*folder*
microfono	*microphone*	**virus**	*virus*
altoparlanti	*speakers*	**stampante**	*printer*
browser/motore di ricerca	*browser*	**scanner**	*scanner*
preferiti	*favorites*	**bianco e nero**	*black and white*

Of course, the list above is not comprehensive, but it is aimed to provide you with the most used/common vocabulary related to the use of a computer.

A few interesting facts about some of these words:

- **Computer fisso** literally means *fixed computer*, as you cannot take it everywhere with you as you would with a laptop! This also explains why laptop is translated as **computer portatile**, *portable computer*.

- Remember that the two verbs **accendere** e **spegnere** have an irregular past participle, **acceso** and **spento**, respectively. Do not hesitate to look at the list of irregular past participles at the end of the workbook whenever you need to do so.

- Yes, the Italian word for your computer *mouse* is the same as in English, whereas the name of the actual animal is **topo**!

- Humorously enough, in Italian when you want to say *black and white*, for example when printing something, so you will say **bianco e nero,** *white and black*.

The last section of this chapter will focus on the vocabulary used for **i social network.** Please note that Italians will usually say just **i social** to refer to social media. Let's look at the vocabulary:

profilo	*profile*	**follower**	*followers*
foto profilo	*profile picture*	**modificare**	*to edit*
pubblicare/postare	*to post*	**condividere**	*to share*
taggare	*to tag*	**cercare**	*to search*
mettere mi piace	*to like*	**filtri**	*filters*
mi piace	*like*	**gruppi**	*groups*
commenti	*comments*	**privacy**	*privacy*
post	*post*	**accedere**	*to log in*
diretta/live	*live*	**uscire/disconnettersi**	*to log out*
storie	*stories*	**chat/conversazioni**	*chat*

Now it is time to highlight some interesting/fun facts about the words:

- The verb **taggare** is used in social media only. For example, if you want to tag an item, the verb you need to use is **etichettare.** The noun **etichetta**, on the other hand, generally refers to a label. In fact, *price tag* is translated as **cartellino**.

- If you think about it, **mettere mi piace** literally means *to put a like*, and we guess that it makes sense, doesn't it? Also, please note that this expression makes sense when talking about social media only. We remind you that the Italian translation of the verb *to like* is **piacere**, which was introduced and discussed in our first workbook Italian Made Easy Level 1.

- The verb **condividere** has an irregular past participle, **condiviso.** If you watched the movie *Into the Wild*, you would probably remember its famous quote *Happiness is real only when shared*, whose Italian translation is **La felicità è reale solo se condivisa**.

- We decided to add this chapter to the workbook not only because we live in an increasingly digital world, but also because the vocabulary we use for this field is commonly used for other sectors that have nothing to do with technology.

- The result? We get **due piccioni con una fava,** an Italian expression whose literal translation – *two pigeons with a bean* – is the equivalent of *two birds with one stone.*

EXERCISES IV

1) **Scrivi la traduzione delle seguenti parole.** *Write the Italian translation of the following IT-related words.*

   a) keyboard　　_____

   b) to edit　　_____

   c) screen　　_____

   d) to like　　_____

   e) laptop　　_____

   f) mobile phone　　_____

   g) calls　　_____

   h) to switch on　　_____

   i) username　　_____

   j) black and white　　_____

   k) airplane mode　　_____

   l) battery　　_____

2) **Cosa pensi dei social?** *What do you think about social media? Write a short text answering the following questions.*

   Ti piacciono i social? Perché?
   Do you like social media? Why?

   Quali social usi più spesso?
   What social media do you use more often?

   Quanto tempo passi sui social al giorno (in media)?
   How much time do you spend on social media per day (on average)?

   Cosa ti piace fare sui social?
   What do you like doing on social media?

   Quali sono i vantaggi e quali sono i rischi dei social?
   What are the advantages and the risks associated with the use of social media?

EXTRA
ITALIAN SONGS

Yes! Our third Italian song!

If you remember, in the first song section we introduced a very famous Italian song, followed by a lesser-known song at the end of Unit 2. In this instance, we chose another very famous Italian song so that we could alternate some great classics and some other beautiful songs that are not well known abroad.

If you think about a famous Italian song, one of the first titles you will think about is probably **Nel blu dipinto di blu**, a song performed by **Domenico Modugno** in **1958**. Does the name ring a bell?

Maybe so. If you go back to the previous song section in Unit 2, you will realize that Domenico Modugno is also the original performer of **Meraviglioso**, whose cover was played more recently by the Italian band called **Negramaro.**

Also, in case **Nel blu dipinto di blu** doesn't ring a bell, it's probably because this song has always been famous under another title: **Volare!**

Well, if you are interested in music, it is worth mentioning that the first time **Nel blu dipinto di blu** hit the stage was during the **Sanremo Music Festival**, which is the most important song contest held every year, in February, in the city of Sanremo (in the Liguria region, where the famous and stunning **Cinque Terre** are). The very first edition of the Festival was held in 1951, and the event has come to its 75th edition in 2025!

Now, let's focus on the lyrics. As usual, we recommend listening to the song first, and then trying to follow the lyrics in Italian. Please look at the translation only after you have completed the first two steps.

 Nel blu dipinto di blu (Domenico Modugno)

Penso che un sogno così non ritorni mai più
I think a dream like this may never come back

Mi dipingevo le mani e la faccia di blu
I painted my hands and face blue

Poi d'improvviso venivo dal vento rapito
Then, suddenly, I was kidnapped by the wind

E incominciavo a volare nel cielo infinito
And I began to fly in the infinite sky

Volare oh, oh
Flying, oh, oh

Cantare oh, oh
Singing, oh, oh

Nel blu dipinto di blu
In the blue-painted blue sky

Felice di stare lassù
Happy to be up there

E volavo, volavo felice più in alto del sole
And I flew, I flew happily higher than the sun

Ed ancora più su
And even higher

Mentre il mondo pian piano spariva lontano laggiù
While the world slowly disappeared far down below

Una musica dolce suonava soltanto per me
A sweet music was playing just for me

Volare oh, oh
Flying, oh, oh

Cantare oh, oh
Singing, oh, oh

Nel blu dipinto di blu
In the blue-painted blue sky

Felice di stare lassù
Happy to be up there

Ma tutti i sogni nell'alba svaniscon perché
But all dreams vanish at dawn because

Quando tramonta la luna li porta con sé
When the moon goes down, it takes them away

Ma io continuo a sognare negli occhi tuoi belli
But I keep dreaming in your beautiful eyes

Che sono blu come un cielo trapunto di stelle
Which are blue like a starry sky

Volare oh, oh
Flying, oh, oh

Cantare oh, oh
Singing, oh, oh

Nel blu degli occhi tuoi blu
In the blue of your blue eyes

Felice di stare quaggiù
Happy to be down here

E continuo a volare felice più in alto del sole
And I keep flying happily higher than the sun

Ed ancora più su
And even higher

Mentre il mondo pian piano scompare negli occhi tuoi blu
While the world slowly disappears into your blue eyes

La tua voce è una musica dolce che suona per me
Your voice is sweet music playing for me

Volare oh, oh
Flying oh, oh

Cantare oh, oh
Singing oh, oh

Nel blu degli occhi tuoi blu
In the blue of your blue eyes

Felice di stare quaggiù
Happy to be down here

Nel blu degli occhi tuoi blu
In the blue of your blue eyes

Felice di stare quaggiù
Happy to be down here

Con te
With you

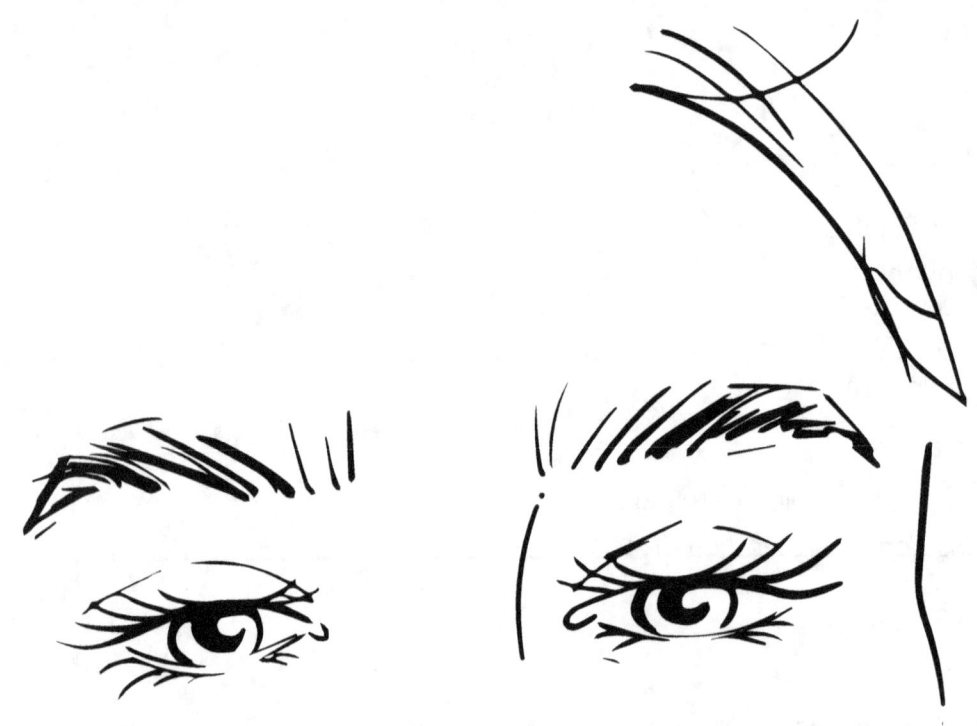

Did you sing? We hope you did!

If you took a closer look to the English translation, you might notice that the lyrics are actually not that difficult in terms of grammar. Probably, the most difficult part is those words that have been tweaked a bit to get a more "poetic" touch. We will tell you more about some of them in the following list of interesting facts/grammar points.

non ritorni: In case you had a doubt on this verb tense, don't worry. It is a tense we have not explained yet, but that we have already mentioned when talking about the imperative mood – **il congiuntivo presente.**

mai più: Literally translated as *never again*, it is used quite frequently. **Example: Non ci andrò mai più**, *I will never go there again!* Please note that those two words – **mai** and **più** – cannot be separated, and you generally find them at the end of the sentence.

Mi dipingevo le mani e la faccia di blu: As it is, the verb **dipingere** – *to paint* – has been used in its reflexive form – **dipingersi**. However, we could also use the "normal" verb and add the possessive adjectives to the direct objects – which are the hands and the face – and the meaning of the sentence would remain the same – **dipingevo le mie mani e la mia faccia di blu.**

Venivo dal vento rapito: As you can see, the translation of this part is *I was kidnapped by the wind*. Even though we have not discussed the passive form in Italian, we can already anticipate that the structure is similar to English, with an auxiliary verb conjugated in the past tense followed by the past participle. In this instance, you can see that the past participle **rapito** has been put at the end of the sentence, but just as a poetic licence.

Incominciavo: Poetic form of the verb **cominciare** – *to begin*.

Continuavo a volare: Please note that the Italian verb **continuare** requires the preposition **a** when it is followed by another verb, as in this instance. However, if it is followed by a noun, a preposition is not needed. **Example: Continueranno le prove nel pomeriggio,** *They will continue the rehearsals in the afternoon.*

Che: A relative pronoun that can be translated as *that* or *which*, as there is no difference between the two words in Italian.

Sé: Don't forget that little accent! In fact, **sé** with the accent is translated as *oneself*, but if you write **se** without the accent, it means *if!*

Svaniscon: Poetic form of the conjugated verb **svaniscono** – *they disappear*. Please note that the verb **svanire** acts like **finire, pulire,** etc. As a reminder, when you conjugate those verbs in the present tense, you will have to add *-isc* between verb root and ending.

Now, are you ready to tackle the next unit?

UNIT 4

EXPERIENCING EVERYDAY LIFE

CHAPTER 1
THE PAST PERFECT TENSE

In the previous workbook, Italian Made Easy Level 1, we discussed the simple past – **il passato prossimo** – and at the beginning of this new workbook we introduced the imperfect tense – **l'imperfetto**. However, there is another commonly used past tense that deserves to be mentioned.

Which tense would you use in English to talk about actions or events that happened before another event in the past?

For example, let's assume that you have already studied this section. This is the corresponding sequence of actions/events that happened in the past: *studying the chapter > doing the exercises*. First, you studied the chapter on the past perfect tense, and then you did the exercises – in other words, studying happened before doing the exercises. This is when you would use the past perfect tense. You would say *I had already studied the chapter on the past perfect tense when I did the exercises*. Here we have two verbs corresponding to two different sentences, joined by *when*.

The first sentence is *I had already studied the chapter on the past perfect tense*, which is also the main sentence as it can stand by itself and make perfect sense. The second clause – *when I did the exercises* – is dependent, as it needs the main clause to make sense.

While the main clause has a verb in the past perfect – *I had studied* – the dependent one has the simple past – *I did*. Why, though?

Because, as anticipated, the sequence of the events is as follows: *You had studied the chapter > you worked on the exercise section*. Two events, one more recent than the other, and both happened in the past. We need to use the past perfect tense for the less recent one.

As you all know, this is how we form this tense in English:

Subject pronoun + simple past of the verb to have + past participle of the main verb

Well, **buone notizie!** *Good news!* In Italian, there is a tense corresponding to the past perfect and it is known as **trapassato prossimo.** In short, whenever you use the past perfect in English, you will use the **trapassato prossimo** in Italian.

As for when you need to use this tense, the "rule" is the same as in English: whenever you are talking about an action or event that happened in the past before another one also in the past.

And this is how you form the **trapassato prossimo** in Italian:

(soggetto) + ausiliare (essere/avere) all'imperfetto + participio passato del verbo principale

The subject pronoun is in brackets because there is no need to mention it – as you already know – unless for some reason it needs to be specified.

The most noticeable difference with the past perfect in English is in the auxiliary verb, because it could be **essere** – *to be* – or **avere** – *to have*. How would you choose one over the other one?

Well, you will just have to apply the same rules we explained when discussing the simple past. Do transitive and intransitive verbs ring a bell? We hope so. However, if you're not sure, we invite you to review the differences between these two group of verbs in the chapter dedicated to the future perfect tense (Unit 2).

Another hint: if a verb needs the auxiliary *to be* for the simple past or the future perfect, it will need it in the past perfect, too.

These are the basics when it comes to the past perfect tense in Italian. Before moving forward, we will show you three examples of verb conjugation in Italian – one requiring the auxiliary *to have*, one requiring *to be*, and the third one will be a reflexive verb. Please look at the table below.

soggetto	**stampare** *to print*	**uscire** *to go out*	**svegliarsi** *to wake up*
io	avevo stampato	ero uscito/a	mi ero svegliato/a
tu	avevi stampato	eri uscito/a	ti eri svegliato/a
lui/lei/Lei	aveva stampato	era uscito/a	si era svegliato/a
noi	avevamo stampato	eravamo usciti/e	ci eravamo svegliati/e
voi	avevate stampato	eravate usciti/e	vi eravate svegliati/e
loro	avevano stampato	erano usciti/e	si erano svegliati/e

As you can see, the verb conjugation in this tense is that bad! It is a mix of different things you have already studied – such as *the imperfect tense* and *the past participle*.

However, it is important to highlight that, in Italian, the auxiliary verb is <u>not</u> conjugated in the simple past – as it is in English – but in the imperfect tense. Do not forget that *to be* is one of the few verbs with an irregular conjugation in the imperfect tense, meaning that the verb root changes radically when we start conjugating the verb.

As you probably remember, whenever we use *to have* as the auxiliary, the past participle does not change. The only thing that you will have to change throughout the verb conjugation is the auxiliary itself (see the example with **stampare**). However, if the verb you are conjugating requires *to be* as the auxiliary, then you will have to change its ending in order to match the gender and number of the subject to which it refers (see the example with **uscire**).

With regard to the past participle, do not forget to check whether the verb you want to use is an irregular one. Always use the list at the end of this book as a reference.

In the table above, we decided to include a reflexive verb just to show you that reflexive verbs are conjugated just like "traditional" verbs. First, we remind you that reflexive and reciprocal verbs always require *to be* as the auxiliary, meaning that the past participle will change to match the gender and number of the subject.

Then, to conjugate a reflexive verb, you must not forget to add the corresponding reflexive pronouns that will go right before the auxiliary conjugated in the imperfect tense.

Now, let's look at a couple of examples with verbs conjugated in the **trapassato prossimo**.

Examples:

- **Aveva faticato molto durante l'anno scolastico prima di cambiare scuola.**
  She had struggled a lot during the school year before changing schools.

In this example, we have a past perfect – **aveva faticato** – and an infinitive – **cambiare**. As you can see, there are two events in the following chronological order: *she had struggled > she changed schools*. As already explained, we must use the past perfect tense for the less-recent action/event, which is, in this instance, the fact that this person had struggled at school.

The verb **faticare** itself is quite interesting. In English, we could translate it either as *to work hard* or *to struggle*. However, these two verbs have two alternative translations in Italian – **lavorare sodo** and **avere difficoltà/fare fatica,** respectively. We can all agree that the meaning of the sentence would change a bit with the wrong translation: in this instance, we translated the verb as *to struggle* because we know the context. As the girl changed school, we can assume that there had been some kind of difficulty before.

- **Visto che avevano perso l'autobus, hanno deciso di tornare a casa.**
  As they had missed the bus, they decided to come back home.

In this example, the clause with the past perfect is the first one – **visto che avevano perso l'autobus** – while the second one has a verb conjugated in the simple past – **hanno deciso di tornare a casa**. This is the sequence of events: *They had missed the bus > they came back home.*

Both verbs – **perdere** and **decidere** – have an irregular past participle – **perso** and **deciso**, respectively. We know that **visto** at the beginning of the sentence may be confusing. If you remember, **visto** is the irregular past participle of the verb *to see* – **vedere**. In this instance, it's a construction corresponding to the English *as/since/give that*.

Please note that we could have switched the order of the two sentences, and the meaning would have remained the same: **Hanno deciso di tornare a casa visto che avevano perso l'autobus.**

One last thing: If you want to form a negative sentence with the past perfect, the only thing you will have to do, as usual, is add a **non** in front of the auxiliary verb.

Example:

- **Non avevamo finito di mangiare quando sei arrivata.**
  We had not finished eating when you arrived.

Please note that, in this example, the main verb of the dependent clause is **sei arrivata**, which is the simple past of the verb **arrivare**. We do not know the subject of the second sentence, but, as the past participle is **arrivata**, we know immediately that the person who arrived was a woman.

 EXERCISES I

1) **Coniuga i seguenti verbi al trapassato prossimo.** *Conjugate the following verbs in the past perfect tense. Please note that there may be verbs with an irregular past participle.*

soggetto	capire to understand	lamentarsi to complain	tradurre to translate
io			
tu			
lui/lei/Lei			
noi			
voi			
loro			

2) **Ricomponi le frasi mettendo le parole nell'ordine giusto.** *Reassemble the following sentences by putting the words in the right order.*

Example: film / il / avevo / di / prima / letto / libro / guardare / il

....Avevo letto il libro prima di guardare il film....
I had read the book before watching the movie.

a) nessuno / festa / non / eravamo / alla / venuti / c'era / ma

_____

We had come to the party, but no one was there.

b) bus / taxi / è / preso / appena / il / arrivato / avevi / un / quando

_____

You had just taken a taxi when the bus arrived.

c) quattro / Londra / prima / vissuto / città / di / a / aveva / diverse / in / trasferirsi

_____

She had lived in four different cities before moving to London.

CHAPTER 2
THE HOUSE, PT. 4

In Unit 3 we explored the vocabulary associated with bedrooms, and now it is time to move on to another room – and quite an essential one... **il bagno** – *the bathroom*!

We are aware that, now that you know the translation for the word *bedroom* – **camera da letto** – it may be tempting to translate this room as **camera da bagno** – which is literally *bathroom* – however Italians simply call it **bagno**.

Actually, **bagno** not only translates the word *bathroom*, but also *bath*. However, this word generally does not create any confusion, because it is quite clear if you are talking about the bathroom room or the action of having a bath. By the way, in Italian, they do not say *to have a bath,* but *to do a bath,* so you would say **fare il bagno** (whether it's in a bathtub or in the sea)!

Also, in Italy, it is quite common to have a bathroom with a washbasin, a bathtub, or a shower, and a toilet. The toilet is almost never in a separate room. Then, of course, some people might have more than one bathroom, but every single one of them will have "the full package."

Now, let's find out the most used words associated with bathrooms:

lavandino	*washbasin/sink*	**shampoo**	*shampoo*
rubinetto	*tap*	**balsamo**	*conditioner*
doccia	*shower*	**bagnodoccia**	*shower gel*
vasca da bagno	*bathtub*	**tappetino**	*bathmat*
gabinetto/WC	*toilet*	**phon**	*hair dryer*
carta igienica	*toilet paper*	**specchio**	*mirror*
bidet	*bidet*	**pettine/spazzola**	*hairbrush*
cestino	*bin*	**spazzolino (da denti)**	*toothbrush*
asciugamano	*towel*	**dentifricio**	*toothpaste*
accappatoio	*bathrobe*	**sapone**	*soap*

Now, as usual, we will tell you some fun facts and additional information on some of the words above:

- The Italian language is quite "practical." For example, in Italian, they do not say *to take a shower*. Why? Because the verb *to take* refers to a manual action of carrying something. This is why, if you say **prendo una doccia** in Italian – which literally means *I take a shower* – you are saying, for example, that you are taking a shower home with you. The right verb to use is *to do* – **fare** – because when you are taking a shower you are performing the action of "doing" it, hence you will have to say **faccio una/la doccia**.

- The word **vasca da bagno** literally means *tub for a bath,* and we guess that it makes sense, doesn't it?

- In every Italian property you will find a **bidet**, and its absence abroad is also one of the most common complaints by Italians! Curiously, it seems that this item, which was first invented in France in the 18th century – and this is why you have to pronounce it as a French word, *bee-deh* – is now very rare in France nowadays!

- If you are staying in a hotel, and you want to request new towels, remember to specify their size – **un asciugamano grande o piccolo** – *a big towel or a small one.*

- Pay attention to the pronunciation of the foreign words used in Italian. **Shampoo** is read as *sham-poh* and not *sham-poo*, while **phon** should be read as *fon*, without exceptions.

- Why do Italians have such a "weird" word for *bathrobe*? Well, there is a specific reason for it. The word **accappatoio** comes from the Latin verb accappare, which means **chiudere in una cappa** in modern Italian – *to close in a "cappa,"* that was an ancient cloak with a hood.

We hope that this chapter will be useful to you, and now it is time to **passare agli esercizi** – *to move on to the exercises!*

EXERCISES II

1) **Scrivi il nome degli oggetti nel bagno.** *Write the Italian names of the items in the bathroom shown in the image below.*

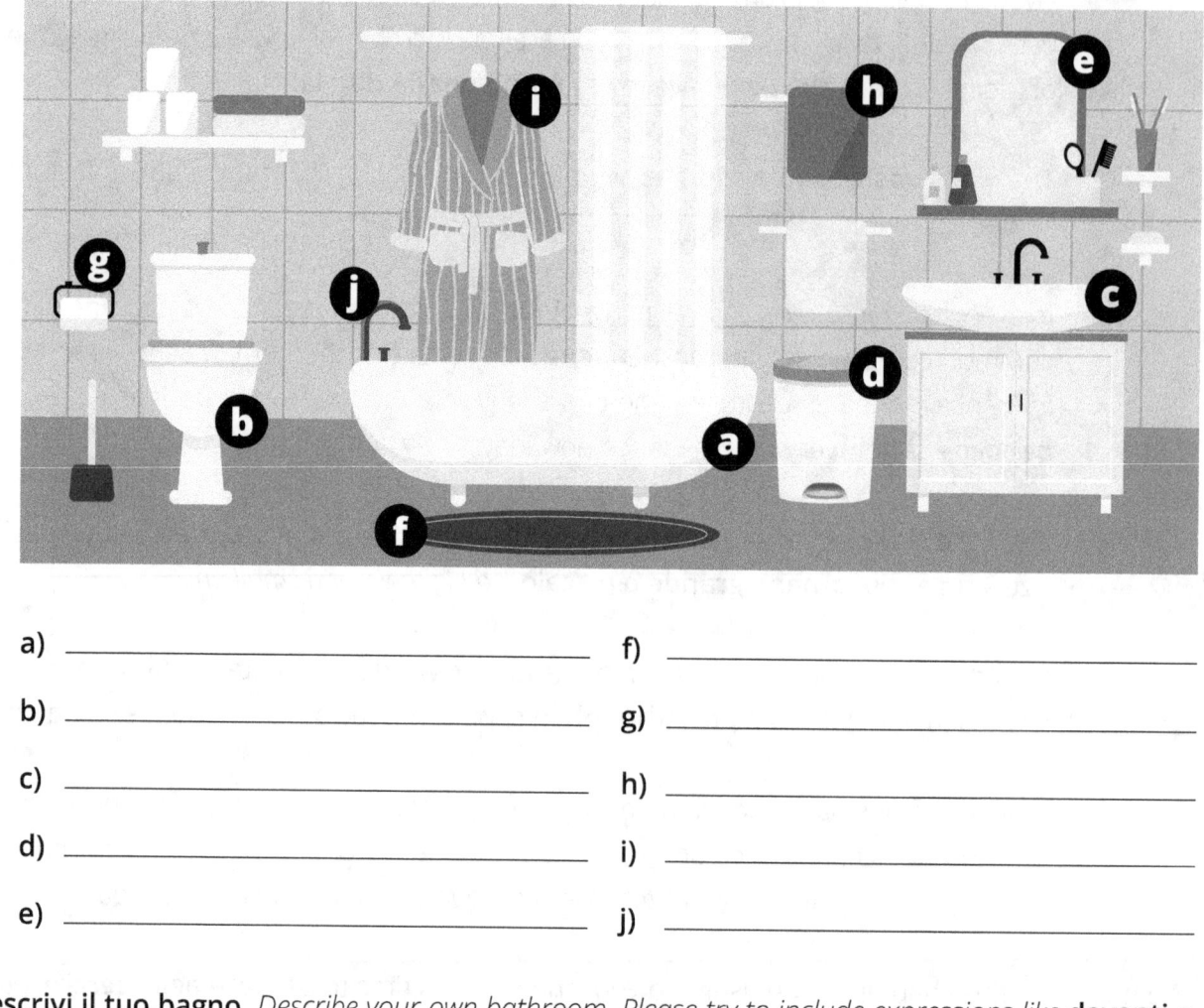

a) _____ f) _____

b) _____ g) _____

c) _____ h) _____

d) _____ i) _____

e) _____ j) _____

2) **Descrivi il tuo bagno.** *Describe your own bathroom. Please try to include expressions like* **davanti a** *(in front of),* **dietro** *(behind),* **accanto a** *(next to),* **a destra di** *(to the right of),* **a sinistra di** *(to the left of).*

_____

_____

_____

_____

_____

_____

CHAPTER 3
ACTIVE AND PASSIVE VOICE

You knew that a grammar chapter was coming, right?

And with this new one, we are going to focus on a very important topic: *the passive voice* – **la forma passiva**.

However, before delving into the world of the passive voice, we should probably discuss what *the active voice* is – **la forma attiva**. Active voice refers to a sentence whose subject performs the action expressed by the verb.

An example of sentence in the active voice could be *They bring the cake to the party*, where they are performing the (very kind) action expressed by the verb, which is *bringing the cake to the party*, in this instance.

On the other hand, a passive voice occurs when the subject becomes the recipient of the verb's action. If we consider the example above, the same sentence in the passive voice would become *The cake is brought to the party by them*.

The new subject of the sentence – *the cake* – is not performing an action directly, but it is subject to the action performed by them.

In English, the subject performing the action is often introduced by the preposition *by*.

Please keep in mind that every passive voice has a corresponding active one, but the same cannot be said for all sentences in the active voice. Only transitive verbs can be used in their active and passive voice. Do you remember how to recognize transitive verbs? If in doubt, do not hesitate to take another look at their definition in Unit 2, Chapter 4, when we reviewed them to introduce the future perfect tense.

Now, let's look at a few examples of sentences in the passive voice and the corresponding active voice.

Examples:

- *Last year, the government was strongly criticized by the citizens.* (Passive voice)
  Last year, the citizens strongly criticized the government. (Active voice)

- *Franco was complimented by the professors on his dissertation.* (Passive voice)
  The professors complimented Franco on his dissertation. (Active voice)

In English, the construction of the passive voice requires the verb *to be* in the appropriate tense and then the past participle of the main verb – as we can see in the two sentences above.

In both examples, we can see the same construction with the verb *to be* conjugated in the simple past. However, if in an active clause there is a verb conjugated in the future tense, you will have to use the future of the verb *to be* and then add the past participle of the verb for the passive voice.

Examples:

- *Francesca will buy a new car next year* (Active voice)
  A new car will be bought by Francesca next year (Passive voice)

- *They will visit a new country in a month* (Active voice)
  A new country will be visited by them in a month (Passive voice)

In short, it is the main verb dictating the tense of the auxiliary verb *to be* in the passive voice.

Now that we have introduced and reviewed how the passive voice works in English, let's move on and find out how to form **la forma passiva in italiano**!

Good news! The concept of passive voice in Italian is the same as in English!

This is how you form the passive voice in Italian:

(soggetto) + verbo essere coniugato + participio passato del verbo principale

The verb *to be* will have to be conjugated according to the tense in the active voice.

Beware! As you will be using the verb *to be* as the auxiliary, do not forget to adjust the past participle according to the gender and number of the subject to which it refers!

Of course, for now, we will focus on the verb tenses you have studied so far. Let's start by looking at a few examples in passive and active voice.

Examples:

- **La medaglia è stata vinta dall'atleta.**
  The medal was won by the athlete.

- **L'atleta ha vinto la medaglia.**
  The athlete won the medal.

- **La decisione sarà presa dal medico.**
  A decision will be made by the doctor.

- **Il medico prenderà la decisione.**
  The doctor will make a decision.

- **La canzone era stata cantata da lui.**
  The song was sung by him.

- **(Lui) Aveva cantato la canzone.**
  He had sung the song.

In the sentences above, you can see different active voices with verbs conjugated in the simple past, future I, and past perfect tense, respectively.

As we have already mentioned, in the English passive voice, the subject performing the action is introduced by the preposition *by*. In Italian, it is introduced by the preposition **da**, as you can see in the examples above.

However, when that preposition is followed by a definite article – as in *by the* – the latter will merge with **da**, thus creating an articled preposition. If you remember, we discussed them in our Italian Made Easy Level 1 workbook.

We decided to add the table below in order to help you review all the articulated prepositions with **da** + definite articles. In case you wanted to refresh your memory, we also included a brief description of how to use them.

| articolo determinativo
definite article | preposizione articolata
articulated preposition (da+definite article) |
|---|---|
| **il**
for masculine singular nouns | **dal** |
| **lo**
for masculine singular nouns starting with S+consonant, PS, PN, GN, X, Z, Y | **dallo** |
| **la**
for feminine singular nouns | **dalla** |
| **l'**
for singular nouns beginning with a vowel | **dall'** |
| **i**
plural of **il** | **dai** |
| **gli**
plural of **lo** and **l'** for masculine nouns | **dagli** |
| **le**
plural of **la** and **l'** for feminine nouns | **dalle** |

You had almost forgotten our beloved articulated prepositions, hadn't you? Well, you can try to avoid them, but they will always come up at some point!

Jokes aside, the passive voice has given us the perfect opportunity to review both the definite articles and the corresponding articulated prepositions, which is great because **repetita iuvant (Latin)** – *repeating is beneficial!*

Examples:

- **Il mistero è stato risolto dal detective.**
  The mystery was solved by the detective.

In this example we can see a passive voice – **è stato risolto**. The subject is *the mystery*, but it is *the detective* performing the main action. The articulated preposition in Italian is **dal**, because **detective** – as most English words used in Italian – is a masculine singular noun, so it requires the definite article **il (da+il = dal)**.

- **Il passivo sarà imparato dagli studenti.**
  The passive voice will be learned by the students.

In this instance, the passive voice has the verb *to be* conjugated in the future – **sarà** imparato. The articulated preposition is **dagli**, as **studenti** is a masculine plural word beginning with *s* + a consonant. If you remember, masculine singular words beginning with that letter combination require **lo** as a definite article, and its plural form is **gli (da+gli = dagli)**.

Besides using the verb *to be*, in Italian there is a second option to form the passive voice. Even if it may seem weird in English, we could also the verb **venire**, *to come*, which will have to be conjugated just like you would do with **essere**.

In case you do not remember it, we remind you that the verb **venire** has an irregular conjugation in the present AND in the future I tense. Please look at the table below for a quick revision:

soggetto	presente *simple present*	futuro semplice *future I*
io	vengo	verrò
tu	vieni	verrai
lui/lei/Lei	viene	verrà
noi	veniamo	verremo
voi	venite	verrete
loro	vengono	verranno

We decided to quickly review these two tenses also because the construction with **venire** for the passive voice can only occur with the present, future, and imperfect tense. You cannot use it with the so-called **tempi composti** – *the compound tenses* – the tenses made of auxiliary + past participle, like the **passato prossimo** and the **futuro anteriore**.

Examples:

- **La camera viene pulita ogni giorno.** *The room is cleaned every day.*
- **Luca verrà creduto dai genitori.** *Luca will be believed by his parents.*

Before finishing this chapter, we should mention one last option to form the passive voice in Italian. We are talking about *the impersonal form* – or the so-called **si passivante**. We know that three options may seem a lot, but it is important to explain all of them so that you can use them and also understand others when they use one of them.

The construction with the **si passivante** is quite common in Italian, and it is used when the subject is generic or represents all of us, *the people*. For example, we may use it when discussing rules, customs, traditions, behaviors, etc.

An important feature of this construction is that there is no actual subject in this kind of sentence. You simply put the **si** followed by the verb conjugated according to the tense you need.

Examples:

- **Non si usa il cellulare a scuola.** *You cannot use a mobile phone at school.*
- **Si vive una volta sola!** *You only live once!*
- **Alla festa si mangerà un sacco!** *We will eat a lot at the party!*
- **Non si sono ancora fatti progressi.** *No progress has been made yet.*

In the examples above, you can see that we have used different tenses with the so-called **si passivante**: simple present, future I, and simple past. You can also see that, as there is no corresponding translation in English, sometimes the passive sentence in Italian can be translated as an active one.

Also, the subjects of those four sentences are not specified, but are rather generic. They either refer to a group of people – **alla festa si mangerà un sacco,** for example, refers to all the people invited to the party – or to general rules – as in **non si usa il cellulare a scuola.**

One last warning before finishing the chapter: please try not to mix the **si passivante** with the reflexive pronoun **si**. For example, if you say **Si sono visti ieri** you are just saying *they met yesterday*, so it is a simple sentence with the reflexive verb **vedersi** in the active voice, conjugated in the simple past.

EXERCISES III

1) **Forma attiva E passiva?** *Mark whether the following verbs have both an active AND a passive voice (AP), or just one active voice (A).*

   a) capire   (to understand)   _____

   b) partire   (to leave)   _____

   c) suonare   (to play)   _____

   d) prendere   (to take)   _____

   e) andare   (to go)   _____

   f) viaggiare (to travel)   _____

2) **Trasforma le seguenti frasi alla forma passiva.** *Change the following active sentences into passive. If there is more than just one option, please write them all. Make sure you conjugate the verbs in the right tense.*

   a) Marco leggeva un libro.

   _____

   Marco read a book.

   b) I fratelli mangiano un hamburger.

   _____

   The siblings eat a burger.

   c) Claudia comprerà un nuovo forno.

   _____

   Claudia will buy a new oven.

   d) Il cane ha preso un giocattolo.

   _____

   The dog took a toy.

   e) Nicola aveva comprato una casa.

   _____

   Nicola had bought a house.

3) Usa il si passivante. *Use the construction with the so-called "si passivante" to write a few sentences about general rules and behaviors at work. Write affirmative and negative sentences.*

Example: Non si dorme al lavoro. *You must not sleep at work.*

CHAPTER 4
WORK AND FESTIVITIES

With this new chapter, we will focus on the vocabulary of a very important field in our everyday life – *work*, **il lavoro**. As days off and holidays are a relevant – *very* relevant, we would say – part of our working life, we decided to add some useful information about the Italian festivities at the end of this chapter.

But let's start with work first. As Italians say, **Prima il dovere, poi il piacere** – *duty first, then pleasure*.

As you all know, there are specific words that we use to describe our work environment, or what we do for a living, and this is why it is important to explore them. The same words can also be used in other fields, so learning them is a win-win situation.

However, we will not focus on the single professions, because we already introduced quite a few of them in our Italian Made Easy Level 1 workbook. Now it is time to deepen what you have already studied and enrich your work-related vocabulary.

Before delving into vocabulary, it may be interesting to know that a full-time job – **un lavoro full time** – in Italy involves around 40 hours of work per week, but a part-time job – **un lavoro part time** – does not necessarily mean working 20 hours per week. In fact, anything below 40 working hours is considered a part-time job.

If you work for yourself, you are a **lavoratore indipendente** or a **lavoratore a partita IVA,** which literally means *a professional with VAT number*, which is an individual tax identification number.

Until 2020, most Italians used to "physically" go to work. Since the pandemic, more and more companies have allowed their employees to work from home, even if for just a few days of the week (of course, it all depends on the job).

Fun fact: You already know that the Italian language has adopted quite a few English words, and to describe the practice of working from home, we do use an English word. However, it is an expression that is not used at all in English-speaking countries! To say *I work from home*, Italians would say **sono in smart working or lavoro da remoto** – *I work remotely*.

Yes, **smart working** is the translation of *working from home* in… a weird mix of English and Italian, we guess? In any case, it is important to learn this definition as it has become a very common one.

If you want to say that you have to go to the office, you will say **lavoro in presenza**.

Now, let's discover a few interesting work-related words:

orario di lavoro	*working hours*
stipendio	*salary*
contratto	*contract*
contratto a tempo determinato	*fixed-term contract*
contratto a tempo indeterminato	*permanent contract*
dipendente	*employee*
datore di lavoro	*employer*
collega	*colleague*
ufficio	*office*
scrivania	*desk*
riunione	*meeting*
sala riunioni	*meeting room*
appuntamento	*appointment*
firma	*signature*
firmare	*to sign*
inoltrare	*to forward*
pausa caffè	*coffee break*
pausa pranzo	*lunch break*
risorse umane	*Human Resources*
disoccupazione	*unemployment*
disoccupato	*unemployed*
curriculum	*resume / CV*
lettera di motivazione	*cover letter*
colloquio di lavoro	*job interview*
progetto	*project*

ruolo	*role*
responsabilità	*responsibility*
fare il pendolare	*to commute*
licenziamento	*dismissal*
licenziato	*fired*
dare le dimissioni	*to resign*
andare in pensione	*to retire*
essere pensionato	*to be retired*
congedo maternità/paternità	*maternity/paternity leave*
anno sabbatico	*gap year*
ferie	*annual leave*
giorno lavorativo/feriale	*working day*
giorno festivo	*public holiday*

We believe we have covered the most important – and most used – words about work. Now, as usual, let's find out more about some of those nouns and expressions:

- Beware! The word **orario di lavoro** is often singular. This means that you will not say *My working hours are...*, but **il mio orario di lavoro è.** We also remind you that the articulated prepositions you should use to say *from... to...* are **dalle... alle...**

  The only exception is for 1 a.m. / p.m., because, in this instance, you will have to use **dall'** and/or **all'**. In case of doubt, we recommend revisiting the chapter focused on telling the time in our first workbook.

  Examples: Il mio orario di lavoro è dalle otto alle cinque – *My working hours are from eight to five;* **Lavoro dall'una alle sei** – *I work from one to six.*

- The Italian word **dipendente** literally means *dependent,* and we guess that it makes sense since your salary depends on someone else, right?

- **Datore di lavoro,** on the other hand, literally means *work giver,* and once again, it sounds quite logical to us!

- Even if the word **collega** ends with an *a* – generally associated with feminine singular nouns – it can be used for both men and women. The difference will be in the article you use: **un/il collega, una/la collega.** Please note that there is a different masculine and feminine form when you switch to the plural – **colleghi** and **colleghe,** respectively.

- **Firma** is a false friend! It does not mean *firm* at all – which can be translated as **azienda, compagnia** or **società** – but *signature.*

- Please keep in mind that, whenever you use the verb *to be*, you need to adapt the following word according to number and gender of the subject to which the verb refers. *I am or we are retired,* then, can be translated as **sono pensionato** or **pensionata** (masculine and feminine singular), **siamo pensionati** or **pensionate** (masculine and feminine plural).

- If you take a closer look, you will realize that **ferie** – always plural – means *holidays/*annual leave but **giorni feriali** means *working days*…? How is it possible that two words coming from the same root mean two completely opposite things? Well, this word comes from the ancient Latin **feriae,** which referred to the day dedicated to the public worship and, on that day, it was forbidden to call assemblies.

  On the other hand, with the spread of Christianity, the same word started to indicate the days of the week – except for Saturdays and Sundays – dedicated to a specific Saint. In short, the Italian noun **ferie** still owes its meaning to the original word in Latin, while the adjective **feriale** refers to the meaning of the same word that spread at a later stage. Funny enough, in French, *jours fériés* still means public holidays! We know. Quite confusing indeed.

We decided to add a short list of all the **giorni festivi** in a year. Remember: Flights and holidays in general are going to be much more expensive if you are traveling on those days!

- **Capodanno** (January 1st), New Year's Day.

- **Epifania** (January 6th), Epiphany Day.

- **Pasquetta** (Easter Monday). Funnily enough, the literal translation is *little Easter!*

- **Festa della Liberazione** (April 25th), celebrating the liberation of Italy from the Nazi occupation.

- **Festa dei Lavoratori** (May 1st), Labor Day.

- **Festa della Repubblica** (June 2nd), Republic Day.

- **Ferragosto** (August 15th), from the Latin feriae Augusti. A holiday established by the emperor **Augustus** in the year 18 B.C.!

- **Tutti i Santi** (November 1st), All Saints.

- **Immacolata** (December 8th), in honor of Mary. It is a widespread tradition for Italian families to decorate their Christmas tree on this day.

- **Natale** (December 25th), Christmas Day.

Speaking of holidays, we believe that there is an interesting Italian tradition worth mentioning! It is the **Epifania**, also known as **la Befana.** Why, though?

Well, it is because on this day, according to tradition, an old (and quite ugly) lady flying on a broom – called **la Befana** – brings treats to all the good children, leaving them inside a stocking. Yes, stockings filled with treats are not common at all for Christmas, but they are popular on Epiphany Day!

She will also leave something for all the naughty children. What, exactly? Coal! That's right. However, to be fair, in most cases it will not be real coal, but a small block of black sugar similar to coal.

Epiphany Day is always a little bittersweet in Italy, because it is also the last day of the Christmas holidays! In fact, a famous saying is **L'Epifania tutte le feste porta via**, that we could literally translate as *The Epiphany takes all the festivities away*.

Now, let's finish this chapter with another very funny Italian saying associated with festivities: **Natale con i tuoi, Pasqua con chi vuoi!** Literally translated as *Christmas with your family, Easter with whoever you want*, it refers to the tradition of spending the Christmas holidays with family, while for Easter, people have "the freedom" to spend it with whoever they fancy.

EXERCISES IV

1) **Traduci le seguenti parole.** *Translate the following words into Italian.*

   a) working hours _____

   b) employee _____

   c) colleagues (masc.) _____

   d) office _____

   e) signature _____

   f) permanent contract _____

   g) HR _____

   h) days off _____

   i) to be retired _____

2) **Ascolta l'audio.** *Listen to the audio file and add the missing words in the text below. The translation of the text will be in the answer key.*

   Lavoro come _____ in un _____ di vestiti a Roma.

   I miei _____ sono dalle _____ alle _____ , tutti i giorni

   tranne il _____ . Io e i miei _____ lavoriamo

   un _____ su due. Ho un _____ e spero che

   diventerà _____ molto presto!

3) Adesso parlaci del tuo lavoro! *Write a short text about your job. Describe what you do, your role, your responsibilities, the working hours, etc. Use as much vocabulary as you can.*

EXTRA
ITALIAN SONGS

The end of a new Unit can mean one thing only: it is time for another **fantastica** Italian song!

This time, we decided to pick a famous song among Italians, but not very well known abroad. It is **Il pescatore** – *The Fisherman* – a short song written and played in 1970 by **Fabrizio De André**, a singer and songwriter who is often described as a poet and a real institution – whether you like him or not!

Without further ado, let's read the lyrics of this beautiful song. As usual, please look at the translation only after listening to the song a first time.

Enjoy!

 Il pescatore (Fabrizio De André)

All'ombra dell'ultimo sole
In the shade of the last sun

S'era assopito un pescatore
A fisherman fell asleep

E aveva un solco lungo il viso
And had a line along his face

Come una specie di sorriso
Like a sort of smile

Venne alla spiaggia un assassino
A murderer came to the beach

Due occhi grandi da bambino
With two big eyes as a child

Due occhi enormi di paura
Two huge eyes filled with fear

Eran gli specchi di un'avventura
Which were the mirror of an adventure

E chiese al vecchio dammi il pane
And he asked the old man "Give me the bread"

Ho poco tempo e troppa fame
I have little time and I am too hungry

E chiese al vecchio dammi il vino
And he asked the old man "Give me the wine"

Ho sete e sono un assassino
I am thirsty and I am a murderer

Gli occhi dischiuse il vecchio al giorno
The old man opened his eyes to the day

Non si guardò neppure intorno
He did not even look around

Ma versò il vino e spezzò il pane
But he poured the wine and broke the bread

Per chi diceva ho sete e ho fame
For whoever said "I am thirsty and I am hungry"

E fu il calore di un momento
And it was the warmth of a moment

Poi via di nuovo verso il vento
Then he went away again toward the wind

Davanti agli occhi ancora il sole
The sun was still in front of his eyes

Dietro alle spalle un pescatore
And a fisherman behind the back

Dietro alle spalle un pescatore
A fisherman behind the back

E la memoria è già dolore
And the memory is pain already

È già il rimpianto d'un aprile
It is the regret of an April already

Giocato all'ombra di un cortile
Played in the shade of a courtyard

Vennero in sella due gendarmi
Two policemen came on horseback

Vennero in sella con le armi
They came on horseback with their weapons

Chiesero al vecchio se lì vicino
They asked the old man if near there

Fosse passato un assassino
A murderer had passed by

Ma all'ombra dell'ultimo sole
But in the shade of the last sun

S'era assopito il pescatore
The fisherman fell asleep

E aveva un solco lungo il viso
And had a line along his face

Come una specie di sorriso
Like a sort of smile

E aveva un solco lungo il viso
And had a line along his face

Come una specie di sorriso
Like a sort of smile

Sooo… Will you become a fan of De André, or maybe his style is not your cup of tea? Well, we hope you at least enjoyed this song! C'mon… Would you have expected to have a fisherman, a murderer and two policemen as the main characters of a song?

Anyway, there are quite a few interesting facts about the lyrics. Keep reading to find out – **continua a leggere per scoprirli!**

assopirsi: Old and more "poetic" verb to say *to fall asleep*. Nowadays, most used is the reflexive verb **addormentarsi**. Oh, speaking of falling asleep… Did you know that Italians almost never use the expression **fare una siesta** – *to take a nap*? The word **siesta** is not that common in Italy. Italians would rather say **faccio un pisolino**.

come una specie di: Very common expression that can be translated as *like a sort of* or *like a kind of*. You can also say **come un tipo di** – which literally translates as *like a type of*.

venne: If you haven't recognized this verb, it is perfectly normal. In fact, it is a verb you are already familiar with – **venire**, *to come* – but in a tense that you have not studied yet, and that we will not cover in this book. It is the so-called **passato remoto** – the "remote" past – another past tense used to describe actions or events that happened a long time ago. However, nowadays, this tense is mainly used in books and newspapers only, and this is why we are not introducing it now.

eran: Verb *to be* conjugated in the imperfect tense – do you remember that it has a very irregular conjugation? The last *-o* of **erano** has been cut as a poetic license.

chiese: Once again, we have another verb – **chiedere**, in this instance – conjugated in the passato remoto tense.

ho fame / ho sete: This is very important. In Italian, you do not say *to be hungry or thirsty*, but *to have hunger/thirst* instead. Well, technically you could say **sono affamato/a** or **sono assetato/a**, but it is way more common to say **ho fame** or **ho sete**. A big plus: **fame** and **sete** are invariable, so you do not have to worry about adapting them – as you would have to do if you are using **affamato** or **assetato**.

dischiuse, guardò, versò, fu: Passato remoto of the verbs **dischiudere** – which is quite an old one – **guardare**, **versare**, and **essere**, respectively.

dietro alle spalle: Here we a have a couple of interesting facts.

First point: In English, *behind* does not require a preposition, and it is followed by its object directly – as in *behind the back*. However, in Italian, it does require the preposition **a**, as if were saying *behind to*.

Second point: Italians do not say *behind the back* – which would literally be **dietro la schiena,** as you learned while studying the chapter on the body parts – but they say *behind the shoulders*. If you remember, **spalle** means *shoulders* indeed.

gendarmi: Old word for policemen. However, this term is still used in some small villages. Nowadays, if you need to call the police – we hope that you won't have to – you will either call **la polizia** (113) or the **carabinieri** (112). As we are talking about useful phone numbers, if you want to call an ambulance, the phone number you should dial is the **118**.

We hoped that you liked this new extra section and, most importantly, that now you feel refreshed and ready to tackle the next – and last – unit of this workbook!

UNIT 5

TALKING LIKE A LOCAL

CHAPTER 1
DEMONSTRATIVE PRONOUNS

If you remember, in Unit 3 we introduced the demonstrative adjectives – **gli aggettivi dimostrativi**. We start this new Unit with a chapter on the demonstrative pronouns – **i pronomi dimostrativi**. *What is the difference?*

There is an important difference. Demonstrative pronouns are just like demonstrative adjectives, but, well... they are *pronouns*. If adjectives modify or specify the noun they refer to, pronouns are used to replace a noun. Let's make it clearer with a couple of examples in English featuring demonstrative adjectives and corresponding pronouns.

Examples:

- *This street is my favorite one in the city.*
  This is my favorite street in the city.

- *Those books are hers.*
  Those are her books.

In both examples, the first sentence shows the use of a demonstrative adjective – *this* and *those* – and the noun they refer to – *street* and *books*, respectively.

On the other hand, if we look at the second sentence of each example, we can now see that the previous demonstrative adjective is not followed by a noun anymore. Instead, *this* and *those* have become pronouns (which are words used to replace nouns). It is as if you were pointing toward those things with your finger. In other words, another *those* used as a demonstrative adjective!

As you can see, the words we used are the same, but with a different meaning. The same will apply in Italian as well. This means that – as you have studied the demonstrative adjectives in Unit 3 – you already know the demonstrative pronouns as well!

Demonstrative pronouns are even easier to remember than the corresponding adjectives. In fact, *this* and *that* must just be adapted according to the subject they are replacing – just like the demonstrative adjectives – but we only have one option for the masculine singular form, one for the feminine singular one, and one for each plural form. Pretty cool, isn't it?

Take a look at the table below:

masculine singular	feminine singular	masculine plural	feminine plural
questo	questa	questi	queste
quello	quella	quelli	quelle

See? We have only four options for *this*, and four options for *that*. That's it.

Compared to the demonstrative adjectives, there is just one little difference, though. Have you spotted it already?

It is the masculine plural form of **quello**. In fact, if you remember, the corresponding demonstrative adjectives for the masculine plural form are **quegli** and **quei,** while the demonstrative pronoun is only **quelli**.

Let's look at a few examples with these pronouns as the subjects of the sentence.

Examples:

- **Quello è mio cugino.** — *That is my cousin.*
- **Questa è la sua macchina.** — *This is his/her car.*
- **Quelle sono le loro scarpe preferite.** — *Those are their favorite shoes.*
- **Quelli sono vecchi jeans.** — *Those are old jeans.*

Please note that we could transform the sentences above in order to use the corresponding demonstrative adjectives. Of course, we would have to add a noun right after the adjective, because this is how demonstrative adjectives work.

Examples:

- **Quel ragazzo è mio cugino.** — *That boy is my cousin.*
- **Questa macchina è la sua.** — *This car is his/hers.*
- **Queste scarpe sono le loro preferite.** — *Those shoes are their favorites.*
- **Quei jeans sono vecchi.** — *Those jeans are old.*

One last thing about the demonstrative pronouns. Not only can we use them as the subjects of a sentence – as in **quella è sua moglie,** *that is his/her wife* – but also as an object!

What do we mean by that?

Let's observe the sentence: **Compriamo questo o quello?** *Shall we buy this one or that one?*

As you can see, **questo** and **quello** are not followed by a noun, so they are pronouns. However, the subject of the verb **compriamo** is **noi**, *we*. This is another use of the demonstrative pronouns, and, in English, we would translate them as *this one* or *that one*. Of course, the same applies to the corresponding plural forms, too.

Examples:

- **Preferisci quelli?** *Do you prefer those?*
- **Voglio comprare questa.** *I want to buy this.*
- **Non prendere quella, per favore.** *Do not take that one, please.*

There is nothing else to say about these pronouns. Shall we proceed with the exercises, then?

 **EXERCISES I**

1. **Completa la tabella.** *Complete the table below with the different forms of the Italian demonstrative pronouns. Please write all the possibilities.*

masculine singular	feminine singular	masculine plural	feminine plural

2. **Completa le seguenti frasi.** *Complete the sentences below with the right form of demonstrative pronoun and / or adjective. If there is more than one option, please write them all.*

   a) Che cos'è _____?
   What is that?

   b) Deciditi: o _____ o _____.
   Make up your mind: either this or that.

   c) Non ho visto _____ serie, ma vorrei vedere _____ sui fantasmi.
   I did not watch this TV series, but I would like to watch that one about ghosts.

   d) _____ alberi sono stati tagliati ieri.
   Those trees were cut yesterday.

   e) I miei fratelli sono _____ con i jeans.
   My brothers are those wearing jeans.

CHAPTER 2
THE HUMAN BODY, PT. 2

If you remember, in Unit 2 we introduced the vocabulary associated with the upper part of the body, and maybe you thought that we had forgotten about the lower part of it?

Well, we have not! In fact, with this new chapter, we will guide you through the vocabulary related to the remainder of our body. One chapter about grammar and one focused on vocabulary, remember?

In the previous chapter on the human body, we stopped at the hips. Now it is time to explore the parts from hips to toes. You will also notice that the list is shorter.

bacino	*pelvis*	**polpaccio**	*calf*
glutei	*glutes*	**caviglia**	*ankle*
sedere	*bottom*	**piede**	*foot*
coscia	*thigh*	**pianta del piede**	*sole of the foot*
femore	*femur*	**dita del piede**	*toes*
ginocchio	*knee*	**alluce**	*big toe*
rotula	*kneecap*		

This list covers the basics regarding the lower part of the body. Now, as we always do, we will highlight a few interesting facts about some of the words above.

- The word **bacino** can mean more than one thing. Not only can it be translated as *pelvis*, but also as *basin, reservoir*. Also, if you remember, the suffix **-ino** is a diminutive one. The result? **Bacino** can also mean *small kiss*. For example, it is quite common for Italians to say **dammi un bacino!** – *give me a small kiss!* – especially when they are talking to children. As you can see, the three translations above are completely different from one another. It is definitely one of the most versatile words in the Italian language.

- The word **coscia** – *thigh* – allows us to review an important rule about plurals. In fact, all feminine singular words ending with **-scia** have a plural ending with **-sce**, meaning that we must eliminate the letter *i* from the ending of the singular form. **Una coscia, due cosce**. Please note that the same does not apply to feminine words ending with **-cia**, as they keep the *i* when becoming plurals. **Example: una camicia, due camicie.**

- **Ginocchio** is another weird Italian word with a masculine singular form, and feminine plural one. **Il ginocchio, le ginocchia.**

- **Dita del piede** literally means *fingers of the foot,* and we guess that it makes sense, but wouldn't it be better to have a different word like in English? Yeah, we agree with you. It would be better, but, unfortunately, there is no other option available.

- Well, there is no "proper" translation for *toes*, but there is one for *big toe*! It is **alluce**, but be careful not to confuse it with **pollice**, which is *thumb*.

✏️ EXERCISES II

1) **Aggiungi i nomi delle parti del corpo.** *Add the names of the following body parts in Italian.*

2) **Descrivi un personaggio famoso!** *Write a short description of a celebrity of your choice. You can also describe a family member or a friend, but please describe them using the vocabulary you learned in the three chapters about upper and lower part of the body, and personality.*

_____
_____
_____
_____
_____
_____
_____
_____

CHAPTER 3
ORDINAL NUMBERS

Are we really going to discuss numbers again?

Yes, we are! In our Italian Made Easy Level 1 workbook, we introduced the numbers, of course, but only the cardinal ones – **i numeri cardinali**. As a reminder, cardinal numbers are *one, two, three, one hundred*, etc.

On the other hand, *ordinal numbers* – **i numeri ordinali** – are used whenever we want to indicate an order of things. For example, *the first, the second, the third*, etc.

As in English, the first ordinal numbers are a bit irregular, and, more specifically in Italian, they are irregular until the 10th. After that, they become regular and very easy.

In terms of use, ordinal numbers need to be preceded by the corresponding definite article. If you think about it, the same applies in English, too, because we say *the second Italian workbook*, for example, and not just *second workbook*.

However, if in English we only have one option when it comes to the definite articles – which is represented by *the* – in Italian, as you all know very well, we have many, so we will have to choose the right one according to the gender and number of the noun to which it refers. More about that in a bit.

To review an important point that we discussed in the first workbook, in Italian, whenever you use a possessive adjective you will need the definite article, too, so a sentence like *our third chapter* would become *the our third chapter* in Italian.

We remind you that the only exception when it comes to possessive adjectives and definite articles is represented by close family members in their singular form. For example, you will have to say **mio figlio**, without the definite article, but **i miei figli**, with the definite article, as we are using the plural form of a close family member (*a son*).

However, if we add an ordinal number in the mix, this exception does not apply anymore. For example, you will have to say **il mio primo figlio** – *my first son* – so now we need the definite article even if it's a close family member in its singular form. In short, forget this exception when you are using ordinal numbers!

Now, let's look at the irregular ordinal numbers from the 1st to the 10th:

1st	primo/prima/primi/prime
2nd	secondo/a/i/e
3rd	terzo/a/i/e
4th	quarto/a/i/e
5th	quinto/a/i/e
6th	sesto/a/i/e
7th	settimo/a/i/e
8th	ottavo/a/i/e
9th	nono/a/i/e
10th	decimo/a/i/e

For each ordinal number, there are four options – masculine singular and plural, and feminine singular and plural. If we take number eight as an example, *the eight* can be translated as **ottavo** (masculine singular form), **ottava** (feminine singular form), **ottavi** (masculine plural), and **ottave** (feminine plural).

Now, what happens after **il decimo numero ordinale**? Well, ordinal numbers become very regular. In order to form them, you will have to take the cardinal number, remove the last vowel, and pick one of the endings among **-esimo/a/i/e.**

Examples:

- 11th **undicesimo/a/i/e** (undici+esim*)

- 35th **trentacinquesimo/a/i/e** (trentacinque+esim*)

- 149th **centoquarantanovesimo/a/i/e** (centoquarantanove+esim*)

    Exception alert! When the unit of the cardinal number is a 3, the *e* will double. For example, you will say **trentatreesimo** for 33th, or **novecentonovantatreesimo** for 993th.

Please note that in Italian, whenever you are telling the date, you must not use ordinal numbers, but the cardinal ones. In short, you do not say *it is the 3rd*, for example, but just *it is the 3* – **è il 3 (gennaio, febbraio, marzo, ecc.)**. Do not forget to pick the right definite article for each number. They are all masculine singular nouns, but remember that there may be some numbers beginning with a vowel… *if you know what we mean*.

Also, as you can see from the examples above, the month goes after the number, and not before. This is why the Italian – and European – date format is the following: day/month/year. For example, you will have to write 3/11 to refer to November 3rd – **il 3 novembre**. If you write 11/3, you will be referring to March 11th – **l'11 marzo**.

Now, before finishing this chapter, let's take a look at a few examples of sentences featuring ordinal numbers, too:

Examples:

- **Il mio primo errore è stato vendere la macchina.**
  My first mistake was selling the car.

This example is an interesting one for a couple of reasons. First, in English, we would use the *-ing* form of the verb – *selling* – but keep in mind that we do not have a corresponding form in Italian. You will just use the infinitive of that verb – **l'infinito**.

The other interesting point of this short sentence is obviously represented by the ordinal number, **primo**. The noun it refers to is **errore**, which is a masculine singular word, and this is why we must say **primo**.

However, if you remember the definite articles – because you *DO* remember them, right?? – the corresponding one for **errore** would be **l'** as it is a noun beginning with a vowel. The definite article, though, now precedes the possessive adjective, so we need to use that one as our reference. In short, it means that we need the masculine singular definite article that we would use for **mio**, which is **il**.

- **Sei davvero stato bocciato per la terza volta?**
  Did you seriously flunk for the third time?

In this instance, the ordinal number in its feminine singular form – **terza** – needs to match **volta**, which is a feminine singular noun. Please note that whenever you want to use *time* in this sense, the word you will have to use is **volta**, and not **tempo** – that we use to refer to *the* time.

Please notice the passive voice **sei stato bocciato,** which in English isn't passive. Now let's move on to the exercises!

EXERCISES III

1) **Scrivi i numeri ordinali in italiano.** *Write the ordinal numbers in Italian. Beware! Write the correct form as indicated (MS-Masculine Singular, FS-Feminine Singular, MP-Masculine Plural, FP-Feminine Plural).*

   a) 16th _____ MS

   b) 2nd   _____ MP

   c) 65th _____ FS

   d) 9th   _____ FP

   e) 43st _____ MP

   f) 88th _____ FP

   g) 100th _____ MS

   h) 3rd   _____ FS

2) **Ascolta l'audio.** *Listen to the audio file and fill in the gaps. You will find the translation of this short text in the answer key.*

Oggi è stato il mio _____ giorno di lavoro! Ero molto _____ perché era un nuovo ambiente, con nuovi _____ . È il _____ lavoro che cambio in _____ anni. Mi sono subito sentito a mio _____, e per fortuna i miei colleghi sono molto _____ . Ho iniziato a lavorare _____ e ho finito _____ .

CHAPTER 4
THE HOUSE, PT. 5

This is the fifth and the last chapter on the house. And our last room will be the living room – **il salotto**!

In Italian houses, there may be a dining room as well – **una sala da pranzo** – but we would say that this room is becoming less common. Most Italians would eat in the kitchen or have a joined kitchen and dining room. In any case, the vocabulary we would use for the dining room is already included in the previous and the current chapters.

Without further ado, let's look at the Italian words associated with the living room:

divano	*sofa / couch*	**quadro**	*painting*
poltrona	*armchair*	**mensola**	*shelf*
tappeto	*rug*	**pianta**	*plant*
cuscino	*pillow*	**cuccia**	*dog bed*
televisione / TV	*TV*	**mobile**	*piece of furniture*
termosifone	*radiator*	**appendiabiti**	*coat hanger*
riscaldamento	*heating system*	**tavolino**	*coffee table*
condizionatore	*air conditioner*	**candela**	*candle*
aria condizionata	*air conditioning*	**pouf**	*pouf*
orologio	*clock*	**radio**	*radio*
caminetto	*fireplace*	**altoparlanti**	*speakers*

Of course, there are other objects that can be found in a living room, but we have already mentioned most of them in the previous chapters.

As usual, we will now add some interesting information about the vocabulary we have just introduced:

- Do not be tempted to pronounce **TV** like in English. In Italian, you will read it as **tivù** – *tee-voo*. The same applies to **radio**, as you have to pronounce it as *rah-dee-oh*.

- If in every Italian room you will find a **termosifone,** the same cannot be said for the **condizionatori.** In fact, AC is not really common in Italian houses. If you are lucky, you may have an air conditioner in one room, but it is very rare to have one in every room of the house, especially in the bedroom. If you're planning on staying in Italy, you can always ask your landlord, even more so if you are traveling to Italy in the hottest months of the year!

- The word **orologio** translates both *clock* and *watch*.

- **Mobile** is definitely a false friend! As you have already studied in the chapter focused on IT (Unit 3), the Italian word for *mobile phone* is **cellulare**. On the other hand, **mobile** can also mean *movable*.

- The word **appendiabiti** literally means *clothes hanger*, and not *coat hanger!*

- The word **pianta** can be translated as *plant* but also *map*, as in *city map* – **la pianta della città**. Also, as we learned in the second chapter of this Unit, the same word can also be used to refer to the sole of the foot – **la pianta del piede**.

- The expression *to have a green thumb* exists in Italian, too – **avere il pollice verde**. On the other hand, if your plants do not survive for more than a week, you can jokingly say that you have **il pollice nero** – *a black thumb*.

- If you remember, we have already said that the suffix **-ino** is a diminutive one. This is why the Italian word **tavolino** literally means *little table*. No coffee involved.

Now that you have read and studied the last chapter on the house, let's move on to the exercises, shall we?

EXERCISES IV

1) **Scrivi il nome degli oggetti nel salotto.** *Write the Italian names of the items in the living room shown in the image below. Please note that there may also be words covered in previous chapters.*

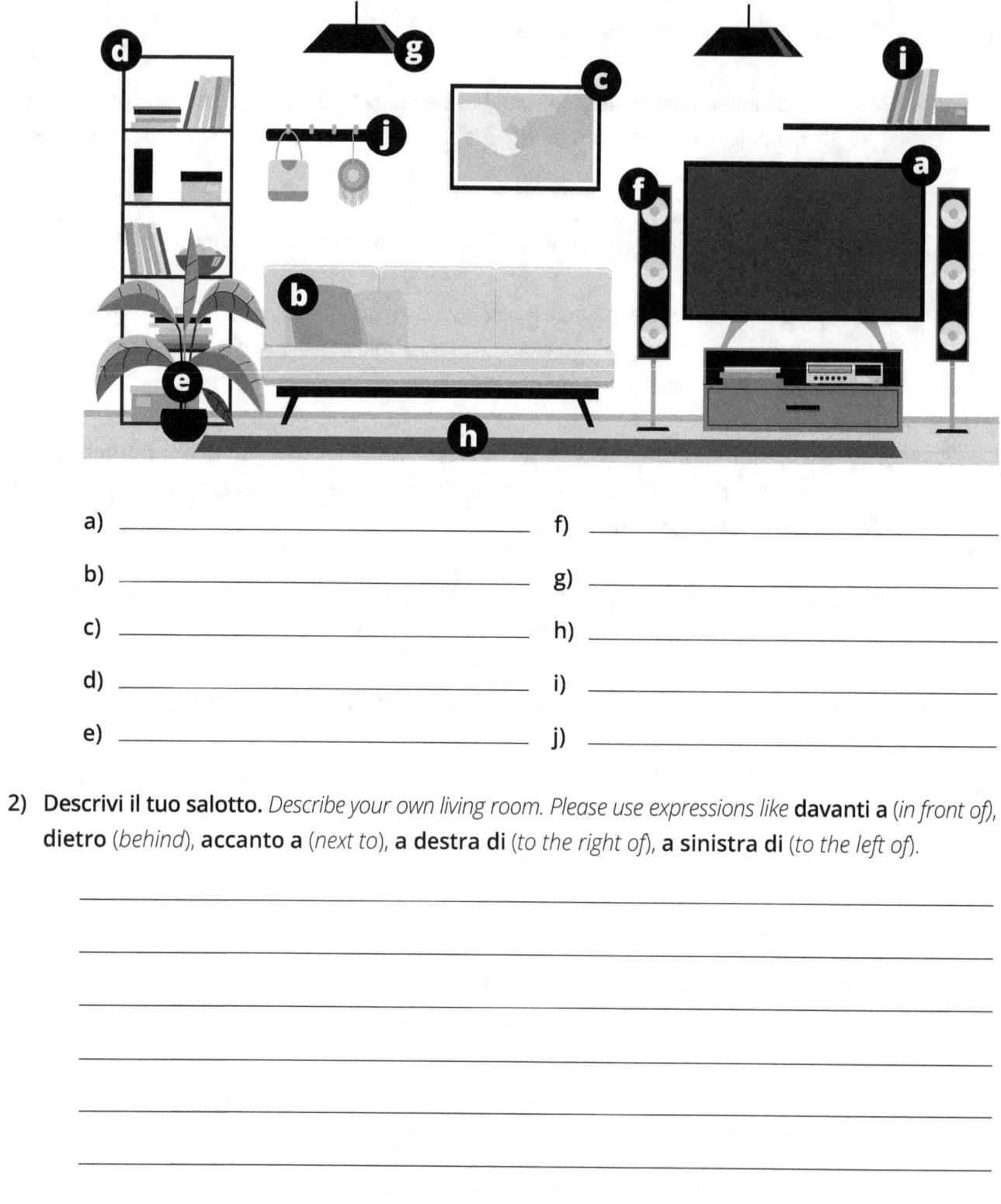

a) _____ f) _____

b) _____ g) _____

c) _____ h) _____

d) _____ i) _____

e) _____ j) _____

2) **Descrivi il tuo salotto.** *Describe your own living room. Please use expressions like* **davanti a** *(in front of),* **dietro** *(behind),* **accanto a** *(next to),* **a destra di** *(to the right of),* **a sinistra di** *(to the left of).*

_____

_____

_____

_____

_____

CHAPTER 5
THE LINGO

Congratulations! You have nearly reached the end of this workbook and this is its final chapter. We have decided to add a funny and interesting chapter about the Italian *lingo* – **il gergo**, *jer-goh* – as you will often hear these expressions when you travel to Italy or speak with a native Italian speaker!

Please note that each region has a different lingo, but there are some common elements. This is why we will focus on those local expressions that will easily be understood everywhere in Italy. Are you ready to explore these words and make them yours?

boh: This is probably the most important word that you should know! Italians use it *all-the-time*. It means *I do not know*, whose "proper" translation would be **non lo so**. **Boh** represents a faster and funnier way to say that you do not know something, and it is literally used by everyone, everywhere in Italy.

Example:

- **Hai superato l'esame?**
  Boh. Lo spero.
  Did you pass the exam?
  I don't know. I hope so.

dai: Another super common and short word that corresponds to the English *come on!*

Example:

- **Dai, vieni con noi!**
  Come on, come with us!

magari: Funnily enough, this is one of the hardest words to master for non-Italian speakers. Why? Because it does not have a corresponding translation in English, although the closest one would be *I wish!* This word could also mean *perhaps*. Depending on the context, it can be sarcastic. Let's examine a couple of examples to clarify this. We will use the same sentence – but with a different conclusion – in order to show you these two possible meanings.

Examples:

- **Esci stasera?**
  Magari! Devo fare i compiti.
  Are you going out tonight?
  I wish! I have to do my homework.

- **Esci stasera?**

  Magari! Ancora non lo so.

  Are you going out tonight?

  Perhaps! I do not know yet.

figurati: This word can be used as a synonym of **prego** – *you are welcome*. In English, it could also be translated as *don't mention it*.

Example:

- **Grazie per il passaggio! Figurati.**

  Thanks for the ride! Don't even mention it.

meno male: Another "difficult" word to master, as there is not a corresponding English word! It can be translated as *how lucky* or *luckily* too. We are going to clarify this with a couple of examples. Please note that this word can also be used in a sarcastic way.

Examples:

- **Meno male che hai preso le chiavi!**

  Luckily you took the keys!

- **Hai un regalo per il tuo compleanno! Meno male!**

  You have a birthday gift. How lucky!

che scocciatura: This expression corresponds to the English *how annoying!*

Example:

- **Ho dimenticato le preposizioni articolate. Che scocciatura!**

  I forgot the articulated prepositions. How annoying!

gufare: A verb belonging to the **-are** groups which literally refers to... *an owl - * **un gufo**!? Well, this verb is a very common one, and has nothing to do with animals. In fact, it means *to bring bad luck / to jinx*.

Example:

- **Oggi c'è la partita. Non la gufare!**
  The match is on today. Do not jinx it!

essere fuori come un balcone: Literally translated as *to be out as a balcony*, it actually means *to be crazy*! Please note that sometimes Italians only use the first part of this expression, without the word balcony.

Example:

- **Vuoi uscire con questo freddo? Sei fuori!**
  Do you really want to go out in this cold? You are crazy!

Non me ne frega niente: Very common expression to say that you do not care at all. Another similar expression would be **non mi interessa per niente/affatto**. However, if you are using this alternative, the structure of the sentence changes a bit. Take a look at the example below.

Example:

- **Non me ne frega niente del calcio – Il calcio non mi interessa per niente.**
  I do not care about football at all.

come te la passi?: This is another way of asking the question *How are you doing?* Please note that this one should be used only with people you know.

Example:

- **Ehi, come te la passi? È da un po' che non ci sentiamo.**
  Hey, how are you doing? It has been a while.

tutto a posto: You can use this expression either as a statement or as a question – **tutto a posto?** Its literal translation in English is *everything in order*, but Italians use it very frequently to say that *everything is alright*.

Example:

- **Come va la vita? Tutto a posto, per ora!**
  How is life? Everything is alright, for now!

sono cavoli amari: A very funny expression whose literal translation is *they are bitter cabbages*... Well, the real meaning of this expression has nothing to do with vegetables. It is a very common way to say that there are big problems ahead.

Example:

- **Non ho studiato. Adesso sono cavoli amari.**
  I did not study. Now it is a big problem.

non costa un cavolo: Yeah... another Italian expression involving a cabbage. Its literal translation is *it does not cost a cabbage.* In this instance, the expression means that something is not expensive at all, probably because cabbages are quite cheap in Italy!

Example:

- **Quella maglietta? Non costa un cavolo.**
  That t-shirt? It is not expensive at all.

come i cavoli a merenda: Seriously, *why are Italians so obsessed with cabbages?* However, in this instance, we are really talking about vegetables. In fact, this expression literally means *like cabbages for an afternoon snack.*

Have you ever eaten a cabbage as a snack? Probably not, and this is the whole point of this expression. Italians use it whenever they are talking about two things that definitely do not go well together!

Example:

- **Il rosso sta bene con il blu come i cavoli a merenda.**
  Red and blue do not go well together.

EXTRA
ITALIAN SONGS

This is our final extra section with an Italian song! We really hope that you enjoyed the others and that we helped you discover a few new interesting songs to maybe add to your playlist.

Since we finished Unit 4 with a classic Italian song, this time we will introduce a more modern song, called **Brividi** – *Chills*, by singer Mahmood and rapper Blanco. This song also won the **Sanremo music festival in 2022** – do you remember? We have already mentioned this festival in the extra section of Unit 3, when we introduced **Nel blu dipinto di blu**.

Speaking of music contests, have you ever heard of the *Eurovision Song Contest?* It is a yearly music competition among all European countries.

Traditionally, the winning act from Sanremo represents Italy at the Eurovision Song Contest, and this is why **Brividi** represented Italy in 2022. Furthermore, the 2022 edition was held in Turin, as in 2021 Italy won with **Zitti e buoni** by the band **Måneskin**... Maybe we will introduce this one in the next workbook. Who knows…? There is only one way to find out ;)

By the way, **Brividi** ended up in sixth place at Eurovision – out of forty participating countries! – so not bad, right? Without further ado, let's discover its lyrics!

 Brividi (Mahmood ft. Blanco)

Ho sognato di volare con te
I dreamed to fly with you

Su una bici di diamanti
On a diamond bike

Mi hai detto sei cambiato,
You told me "You have changed"

Non vedo più la luce nei tuoi occhi
I can't see a light in your eyes anymore

La tua paura cos'è?
What is your fear?

Un mare dove non tocchi mai
A sea where you never touch the bottom

Anche se il sesso non è
Even if sex is not

La via di fuga dal fondo
A real escape route

Dai, non scappare da qui
Come on, do not run away from here

Non lasciarmi così
Do not leave me like this

Nudo con i brividi
Naked with the chills

A volte non so esprimermi
Sometimes I do not know how to express myself

E ti vorrei amare, ma sbaglio sempre
And I would like to love you, but I always make mistakes

E ti vorrei rubare un cielo di perle
And I would like to steal a sky of pearls for you

E pagherei per andar via,
And I would pay to go away,

Accetterei anche una bugia
I would even accept a lie

E ti vorrei amare, ma sbaglio sempre
And I would like to love you, but I always make mistakes

E mi vengono i brividi, brividi, brividi
And I got the chills, the chills, the chills

Tu, che mi svegli il mattino
You, waking me up in the morning

Tu, che sporchi il letto di vino
You, spilling wine in bed

Tu, che mi mordi la pelle
You, biting my skin

Con i tuoi occhi da vipera
With your snakelike eyes

E tu, sei il contrario di un angelo
And you, you are the opposite of an angel

E tu, sei come un pugile all'angolo
And you, you are like a boxer in the corner

E tu scappi da qui, mi lasci così
And you run away from here, you leave me like this

Nudo con i brividi
Naked with the chills

A volte non so esprimermi
Sometimes I do not know how to express myself

E ti vorrei amare, ma sbaglio sempre
And I would like to love you, but I always make mistakes

E ti vorrei rubare un cielo di perle
And I would like to steal a sky of pearls for you

E pagherei per andar via,
And I would pay to go away,

Accetterei anche una bugia
I would even accept a lie

E ti vorrei amare, ma sbaglio sempre
And I would like to love you, but I always make mistakes

E mi vengono i brividi, brividi, brividi
And I got the chills, the chills, the chills

Dimmi che non ho ragione
Tell me that I am not right

Vivo dentro una prigione
I live in a prison

Provo a restarti vicino
I try to stay close to you

Ma scusa se poi rovino tutto
I am sorry if I ruin everything

Non so dirti ciò che provo, è un mio limite
I do not know how to tell you what I feel, it is a limit of mine

Per un ti amo ho mischiato droghe e lacrime
For an "I love you," I mixed drugs and tears

Questo veleno che ci sputiamo ogni giorno
This venom that we spit at each other every day

Io non lo voglio più addosso
I do not want it anymore

Lo vedi, sono qui,
You see, I am here,

Su una bici di diamanti, uno fra tanti.
On a diamond bike, one among many.

Nudo con i brividi
Naked with the chills

A volte non so esprimermi
Sometimes I do not know how to express myself

E ti vorrei amare, ma sbaglio sempre
And I would like to love you, but I always make mistakes

E ti vorrei rubare un cielo di perle
And I would like to steal a sky of pearls for you

E pagherei per andar via,
And I would pay to go away,

Accetterei anche una bugia
I would even accept a lie

E ti vorrei amare, ma sbaglio sempre
And I would like to love you, but I always make mistakes

E mi vengono i brividi, brividi, brividi
And I got the chills, the chills, the chills

We hope that this beautiful song gave you the chills for real! Also, we have a nice surprise for you, as we approach the end of this workbook. No more grammar or vocabulary on this song! Just enjoy it and sing along. Hopefully, you will discover more Italian songs – there is a whole world waiting for you!

CONCLUSION

Ce l'hai fatta! *You made it!*

Now it is truly the end of our Italian Made Easy Level 2 workbook. We really hope that you enjoyed this journey into the Italian language, and that now you are more motivated than ever to continue. However, **ancora non è finita!** *It is not over yet!*

You still have a few steps to take in order to master this beautiful language, and we want to thank you for choosing us as your travel companions.

We know that learning a new language is not easy, but **guardati indietro** – *look behind you*. You have learned so much already! Now you are able to talk in Italian in the present, in the past, and in the future tense. It is a lot, and you should definitely be proud of yourself.

As we have already done for our first workbook, we want to give you some advice to make the most out of this learning experience and to keep on improving your skills:

- The most important thing, when learning a new language, is *consistency*. You have finished this book, but please do not stop practicing. Of course, feel free to take a (short) break. But keep on including this new language in your daily routine. Even 10 minutes per day are beneficial. We are not saying that you should read a whole book in Italian, or that you should keep on studying every single day.

  You can also watch short videos in Italian, listen to a podcast maybe, or even watch an Italian TV series with English subtitles. In fact, if you do decide to watch an Italian TV series, you should **andare per gradi** – *go one step at a time*. Start with subtitles in English first, and then switch to the Italian ones as soon as you feel comfortable enough.

- Most importantly, do not focus on one skill only. You have to practice *all of them*. It means that you should read, listen, speak, and write in Italian. Some people find that the hardest skill is listening, others think that speaking is the most difficult skill. Everyone is different, but that does not mean you should focus on that one thing that you find easiest. It is quite the opposite. Focus on the most difficult skills in order to overcome your weaknesses – because you can and you will improve your Italian.

- You will make mistakes – no doubt you will make some, and it is also perfectly normal. **Dai,** you are already talking in another language. Basically, you're already a superhero! This is why you should not be afraid to go for it when you speak in Italian. **Gli errori sono i tuoi migliori insegnanti.** *Mistakes are your best teachers.*

- Learning a new language always requires *time* – for everyone! That means one thing only: you must be *patient* – **devi essere paziente**. Remember that right now you are adding a lot of bricks to the foundations you built when you started to learn this beautiful language. As the Italians say, **la fretta è cattiva consigliera** – meaning that *haste is a poor advisor*, and this saying applies to languages as well. It is better to learn little by little than doing massive full immersions to try to speed up the process.

Grazie ancora, e a presto!
Thanks again, and see you soon!

ILLUSTRATED GUIDE TO ITALIAN GESTURES

The goal of this illustrated guide is to show you some of the most common Italian gestures. Of course, do not expect all Italians to use them all the time. However, on the other hand, every single Italian will understand if you decide to use one of the gestures below!

Learn the gestures like a real Italian, and you will see how handy they can be, especially if you forget how to say something and you would like to reply in a simple – yet clearly understandable – way.

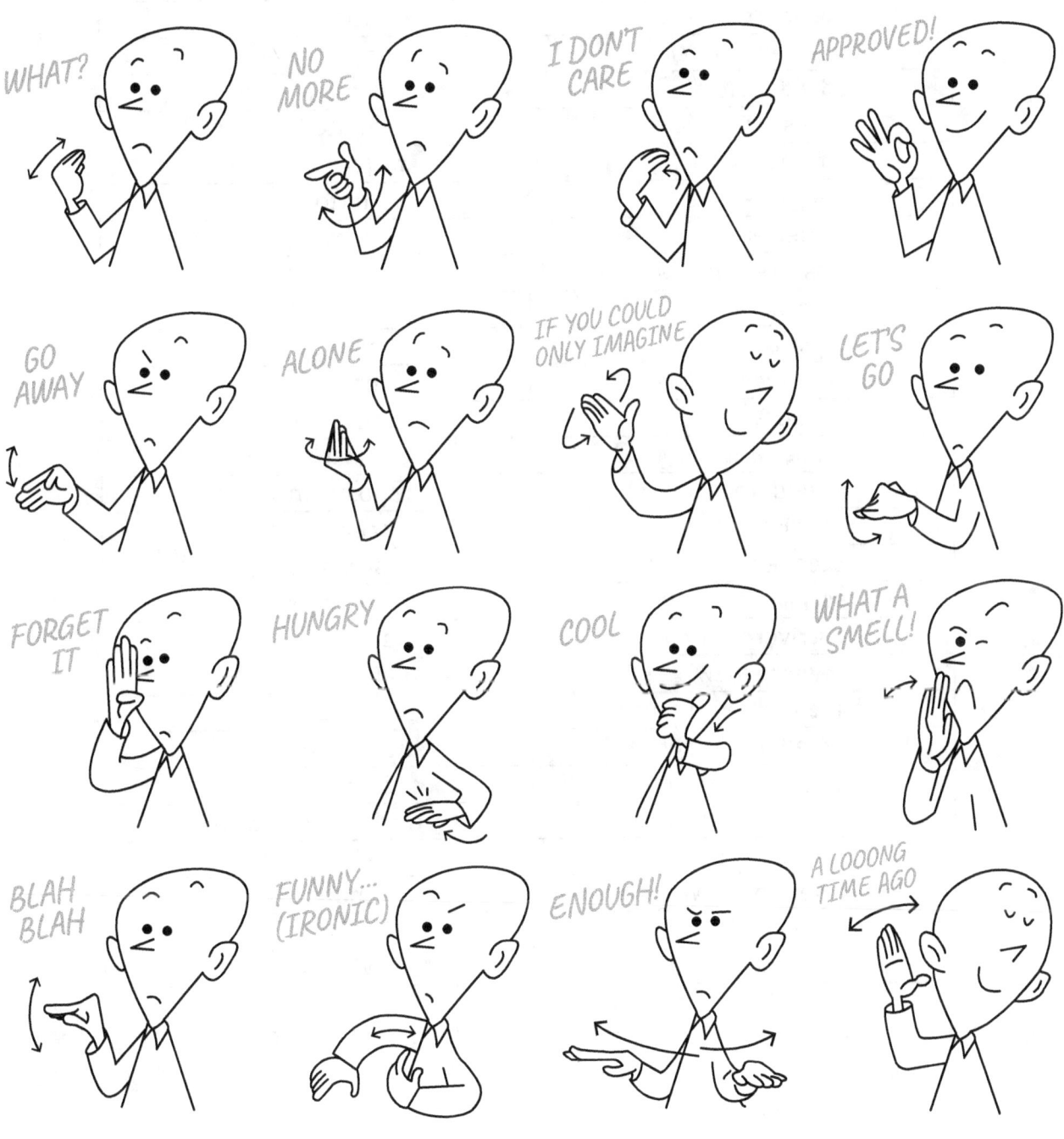

IRREGULAR PAST PARTICIPLES

Infinito *infinitive*	participio passato *past participle*
aprire *to open*	**aperto** *opened*
accendere *to switch on*	**acceso** *switched on*
bere *to drink*	**bevuto** *drunk*
chiedere *to ask*	**chiesto** *asked*
chiudere *to close*	**chiuso** *closed*
correre *to run*	**corso** *run*
decidere *to decide*	**deciso** *decided*
dire *to say/tell*	**detto** *said/told*
dividere *to divide*	**diviso** *divided*
essere *to be*	**stato** *been*
fare *to do/make*	**fatto** *done/made*
leggere *to read*	**letto** *read*
mettere *to put*	**messo** *put*
nascere *to be born*	**nato/a** *born*
perdere *to lose*	**perso** *lost*
piangere *to cry*	**pianto** *cried*
prendere *to take*	**preso** *taken*
ridere *to laugh*	**riso** *laughed*
rimanere *to stay*	**rimasto** *stayed*
rispondere *to answer*	**risposto** *answered*
scegliere *to choose*	**scelto** *chosen*
scendere *to get off*	**sceso** *got off*
scoprire *to find out*	**scoperto** *found out*
scrivere *to write*	**scritto** *written*
spegnere *to switch off*	**spento** *switched off*
spendere *to spend – money*	**speso** *spent*
succedere *to happen*	**successo** *happened*
togliere *to take off*	**tolto** *taken off*
tradurre *to translate*	**tradotto** *translated*
vedere *to see*	**visto** *seen*
venire *to come*	**venuto** *come*
vivere *to live*	**vissuto** *lived*
vincere *to win*	**vinto** *won*

Please note that this is not a comprehensive list of all the irregular Italian verbs. The verbs in the table above are just those more common. We do not want you to feel overwhelmed and, most importantly, we want to give you all the tools you need to start practicing and speaking right away!

FALSE FRIENDS

One last thing before finishing our second workbook on the Italian language. We thought that it would be useful – and funny – to add a short list of the most common false friends in Italian. **Fai attenzione a queste parole!** *Beware of these words!*

addetto	*assigned (addicted is* **dipendente***)*
allegato	*attachment (allegation is* **accusa***)*
annoiarsi	*to get bored (to annoy is* **infastidire***)*
argomento	*topic (argument is* **litigio** *or* **discussione***)*
attendere	*to wait (to attend is* **partecipare***)*
attualmente	*currently (actually is* **a dire il vero***)*
bravo	*good, clever (brave is* **coraggioso***)*
calamita	*magnet (calamity is* **calamità***)*
caldo	*hot (cold is* **freddo***)*
camera	*room (camera is* **macchina fotografica***)*
cantina	*cellar (canteen is* **mensa***)*
collera	*rage (no diseases involved)*
confrontare	*to compare (to confront is* **affrontare***)*
conveniente	*good value (convenient is* **comodo***)*
delusione	*disappointment (delusion is* **illusione***)*
educazione	*politeness (education is* **istruzione***)*
estate	*summer (estate is* **proprietà***)*
fattoria	*farm (factory is* **fabbrica***)*
grosso	*big (gross is* **disgustoso***)*
libreria	*bookshop (library is* **biblioteca***)*
magazzino	*warehouse (magazine is* **rivista***)*
morbido	*soft (morbid is* **morboso***)*

parenti	*relatives (parents* is **genitori**)
pretendere	*to demand (to pretend* is **fingere**)
ricordo	*a memory (record* is **nota**)
rumore	*noise (rumour* is **pettegolezzo**)
stampa	*print (stamp* is **francobollo**)

ANSWER KEY
UNIT 1

Exercises I

1)
a) asciugando
b) chiamando
c) bevendo
d) guardando
e) finendo
f) avendo
g) facendo
h) scrivendo
i) sentendo

2)
a) to dry
b) to call
c) to drink
d) to watch
e) to end
f) to have
g) to do/make
h) to write
i) to hear

3) *The exercise involves the ability to use the present progressive based on the information learned so far.*

Exercises II

1)
a) studio
b) camera da letto
c) sala da pranzo
d) salotto
e) bagno
f) cucina

2) Finalmente **abbiamo comprato** casa! Eravamo **in affitto** da ormai cinque anni. Avevamo un **monolocale** molto carino in centro, non lontano dalla stazione. Anche se non era **grandissimo**, ci siamo sempre sentiti a casa. Ora che la mia ragazza è incinta, ci serviva un'altra **camera da letto**. Il mio sogno è sempre stato quello di avere un **giardino**, e sono davvero contento che la nostra nuova casa lo abbia! **Non vedo l'ora** di trasferirci.

Translation

We finally bought a house! We had been renting for five years. We had a very nice studio in the city center, not far from the train station. Even if it was not very big, we have always felt at home. Now that my girlfriend is pregnant, we needed another bedroom. My dream has always been having a garden, and I am really glad that our new house has one! I am looking forward to moving.

3) *The exercise involves the ability to use all the information learned so far.*

Exercises III

1)
a) I
b) SP
c) SP I
d) SP
e) I
f) SP
g) SP

2)

soggetto	sedersi to sit	vendere to sell	essere to be	fermare to stop
io	mi sedevo	vendevo	ero	fermavo
tu	ti sedevi	vendevi	eri	fermavi
lui/lei/Lei	si sedeva	vendeva	era	fermava
noi	ci sedevamo	vendevamo	eravamo	fermavamo
voi	vi sedevate	vendevate	eravate	fermavate
loro	si sedevano	vendevano	erano	fermavano

3) Quando **ero** un adolescente, **volevo** imparare l'inglese a ogni costo. **Sapevo** che mi sarebbe **stato** utile, e in più **amavo** viaggiare. **Speravo** di riuscire a farmi capire ovunque andassi. **Ho studiato** sodo ogni giorno, e devo ammettere che non è stato facile. Iniziavo la mattina e **finivo** la sera, esausto. **Posso** dire di essere molto fiero di me perché adesso **parlo** benissimo l'inglese.

Exercises IV

The two exercises involve the ability to use all the information learned so far.

UNIT 2

Exercises I

1)

soggetto	cucinare	lanciare	credere	essere
io	cucinerò	lancerò	crederò	sarò
tu	cucinerai	lancerai	crederai	sarai
lui/lei/Lei	cucinerà	lancerà	crederà	sarà
noi	cucineremo	lanceremo	crederemo	saremo
voi	cucinerete	lancerete	crederete	sarete
loro	cucineranno	lanceranno	crederanno	saranno

2)
a) I will start **comincerò**.
b) We will run **correremo**.
c) You will kiss **bacerai**.
d) You will come **verrete**.
e) I will write **scriverò**.
f) She will have **avrà**.
g) He will pray **pregherà**.

3) *The exercise involves the ability to use all the information learned so far.*

Exercises II

1)
a) microonde
b) caffettiera/moka
c) sedia
d) tostapane
e) frigorifero
f) fornelli
g) lavandino
h) pentola
i) tazza
j) coltello

2) *The exercise involves the ability to use all the information learned so far.*

Exercises III

1)

coraggioso	**codardo**
buono	cattivo
estroverso	timido
sensibile	**insensibile**
egoista	**altruista**
chiacchierone	taciturno
felice	**triste**
bugiardo	**sincero**
simpatico	antipatico

2) *The exercise involves the ability to use all the information learned so far.*

Exercises IV

1)

soggetto	**lavare** to wash	**scrivere** to write	**essere** to be
io	avrò lavato	avrò scritto	sarò stato/a
tu	avrai lavato	avrai scritto	sarai stato/a
lui/lei/Lei	avrà lavato	avrà scritto	sarà stato/a
noi	avremo lavato	avremo scritto	saremo stati/e
voi	avrete lavato	avrete scritto	sarete stati/e
loro	avranno lavato	avranno scritto	saranno stati/e

2) Tra cinque anni **avrò trovato** sicuramente un lavoro che **mi piace**! **Ho studiato** per diventare un ingegnere, e **mi sono laureato** un mese fa. Spero di **incontrare** dei colleghi simpatici e **in gamba**, e di **affittare** un appartamento accogliente. Ah, tra cinque anni, io e la mia compagna **saremo diventati** genitori!

Exercises V

1)
   a) occhio
   b) naso
   c) mano
   d) bocca
   e) stomaco
   f) capelli
   g) orecchio
   h) collo
   i) braccio

2) *The exercise involves the ability to use all the information learned so far.*

UNIT 3

Exercises I

1)

masculine singular	feminine singular	masculine plural	feminine plural
questo quest'	questa quest'	questi	queste
quello quel quell'	quella quell'	quegli quei	quelle

2)   a) Che cos'è **questo** caos?
       b) **Quella** macchina laggiù è molto costosa.
       c) I nostri figli sono **quei** ragazzi con la maglietta blu.
       d) **Quest'anno** andranno negli Stati Uniti.
       e) Adoro **queste** casette! Spero di comprarne una.
       f) **Quel** videogioco gli è piaciuto molto.
       g) **Quegli** uffici sono grandi, ma non sono in centro.

Exercises II

1)   a) armadio   f) cuscino
       b) scrivania   g) sedia
       c) pavimento   h) tappeto
       d) orologio   i) lenzuolo
       e) persiana   j) tende

2) *The exercise involves the ability to use all the information learned so far.*

Exercises III

1)

soggetto	guardare *to watch*	pentirsi *to regret*	scrivere *to write*
tu	**guarda!**	**pentiti!**	**scrivi!**
Lei	guardi!	si penta!	scriva!
noi	**guardiamo!**	**pentiamoci!**	**scriviamo!**
voi	**guardate!**	**pentitevi!**	**scrivete!**
loro	guardino!	si pentano!	scrivano!

2) a) He is in the classroom **non correre!**
    b) We are at the restaurant **mangiamo!**
    c) You have an exam **studia!**
    d) He is late **muoviti!**
    e) You are hungry **cucinate!**
    f) He is angry **calmati!**

Exercises IV

1) a) tastiera
    b) modificare
    c) schermo
    d) mettere mi piace
    e) computer portatile
    f) cellulare
    g) chiamate
    h) accendere
    i) nome utente
    j) bianco e nero
    k) modalità aereo
    l) batteria

2) *The exercise involves the ability to use all the information learned so far.*

UNIT 4

Exercises I

1)

soggetto	capire *to understand*	lamentarsi *to complain*	tradurre *to translate*
io	avevo capito	mi ero lamentato/a	avevo tradotto
tu	avevi capito	ti eri lamentato/a	avevi tradotto
lui/lei/Lei	aveva capito	si era lamentato/a	aveva tradotto
noi	avevamo capito	ci eravamo lamentati/e	avevamo tradotto
voi	avevate capito	vi eravate lamentati/e	avevate tradotto
loro	avevano capito	si erano lamentati/e	avevano tradotto

2) a) Eravamo venuti alla festa, ma non c'era nessuno.

b) Avevi appena preso un taxi quando è arrivato il bus.
Other possible answers: Avevi appena preso un taxi quando il bus è arrivato; Quando il bus è arrivato avevi appena preso un taxi.

c) Aveva vissuto in quattro città diverse prima di trasferirsi a Londra.
Another possible answer: Prima di trasferirsi a Londra aveva vissuto in quattro città diverse.

Exercises II

1)
a) vasca da bagno
b) gabinetto/WC
c) lavandino
d) cestino
e) specchio
f) tappetino
g) carta igienica
h) asciugamano
i) accappatoio
j) rubinetto

2) *The exercise involves the ability to use all the information learned so far.*

Exercises III

1)
   a) AP
   b) A
   c) AP
   d) AP
   e) A
   f) A

2)
   a) Un libro era letto da Marco; un libro veniva letto da Marco.
   b) Un hamburger è mangiato dai fratelli; un hamburger viene mangiato dai fratelli.
   c) Un nuovo forno sarà comprato da Claudia; un nuovo forno verrà comprato da Claudia.
   d) Un giocattolo è stato preso dal cane.
   e) Una casa era stata comprata da Nicola.

3) *The exercise involves the ability to use all the information learned so far.*

Exercises IV

1)
   a) orario di lavoro
   b) dipendente
   c) colleghi
   d) ufficio
   e) firma
   f) contratto a tempo indeterminato
   g) risorse umane
   h) ferie
   i) essere pensionato/a/i/e

2) Lavoro come **commesso** in un **negozio** di vestiti a Roma. I miei **orari di lavoro** sono dalle **dieci** alle **sei**, tutti i giorni tranne il **fine settimana**. Io e i miei **colleghi** lavoriamo un **sabato** su due. Ho un **contratto a tempo determinato** e spero che diventerà **indeterminato** molto presto!

Translation

I work as a shop assistant in a clothing store in Rome. My working hours are from ten to six every day except in the weekend. My colleagues and I work every other Saturday. I have a fixed-term contract, and I hope it will become permanent very soon!

3) *The exercise involves the ability to use all the information learned so far.*

UNIT 5

Exercises I

1)

masculine singular	feminine singular	masculine plural	feminine plural
questo	questa	questi	queste
quello	quella	quelli	quelle

2)   a) Che cos'è **quello/quella**?
          b) Deciditi: o **questo/questa** o **quello/quella**.
          c) Non ho visto **questa** serie, ma vorrei vedere **quella** sui fantasmi.
          d) **Quegli** alberi sono stati tagliati ieri.
          e) I miei fratelli sono **quelli** con i jeans.

Exercises II

1)   a) coscia
          b) ginocchio
          c) dita del piede
          d) polpaccio
          e) caviglia
          f) piede

2) *The exercise involves the ability to use all the information learned so far.*

Exercises III

1)   a) sedicesimo
          b) secondi
          c) sessantacinquesima
          d) none
          e) quarantatreesimi
          f) ottantottesime
          g) centesimo
          h) terza

2) Oggi è stato il mio **primo** giorno di lavoro! Ero molto **nervoso** perché era un nuovo ambiente, con nuovi **colleghi**. È il **terzo** lavoro che cambio in **sette** anni. Mi sono subito sentito a mio **agio**, e per fortuna i miei colleghi sono molto **simpatici**. Ho iniziato a lavorare **alle otto** e ho finito **alle sei**.

Translation

Today was my first day of work! I was very nervous because it was a new environment, with new colleagues. It is the third job I have changed in seven years. I felt immediately at ease, and luckily my colleagues are really nice. I started working at eight and finished at six.

Exercises IV

1)
- a) televisione / TV
- b) cuscino
- c) quadro
- d) libreria
- e) pianta
- f) altoparlanti
- g) lampadario
- h) tappeto
- i) libri
- j) appendiabiti

2) *The exercise involves the ability to use all the information learned so far.*

MORE BOOKS BY LINGO MASTERY

We are not done teaching you Italian until you're fluent!

Here are some other titles you might find useful in your journey of mastering Italian:

✓ Italian Short Stories for Beginners

✓ Intermediate Italian Short Stories

✓ 2000 Most Common Italian Words in Context

✓ Conversational Italian Dialogues

But we have many more!

Check out all of our titles at **www.lingomastery.com/italian**

www.ingramcontent.com/pod-product-compliance
Lightning Source LLC
Chambersburg PA
CBHW081448070526
44586CB00019B/2273